Consumer Research For Management Decisions

MELVIN PRINCE
Director of Research
Marsteller, Inc.

with the collaboration of
IRENE A. SILBERT

A RONALD PRESS PUBLICATION
JOHN WILEY & SONS
New York • Chichester • Brisbane • Toronto • Singapore

Library of Congress Cataloging in Publication Data:

Prince, Melvin.
    Consumer research for management decisions.

    (Ronald series on marketing management, ISSN
0275-875X)
    "A Ronald Press publication."
    Bibliography: p.
    Includes index.

    1. Consumers—Research.   2. Marketing research.
I. Silbert, Irene A.   II. Title.   III. Series.
HF5415.3.P74   658.8'34   81-16509
ISBN 0-471-09715-2   AACR2

*Methodology can make a direct contribution to
the advancement of our knowledge of human
affairs, inasmuch as it provides organizing
principles by which such knowledge can be
organized and codified.*

Paul F. Lazarsfeld

Series Editor's Foreword

Marketing management is among the most dynamic of the business functions. On the one hand it reflects the everchanging marketplace and the constant evolution of customer preferences and buying habits, and of competition. On the other hand, it grows continually in sophistication and complexity as developments in management science are applied to the work of the marketing manager. If he or she is to be a true management professional, the marketing person must stay informed about these developments.

The Ronald Series on Marketing Management has been developed to serve this need. The books in the series have been written for managers. They combine a concern for management application with an appreciation for the relevance of developments in such areas of management science as behavioral science, financial analysis, mathematical modeling, and research methodology, as well as the insights gained from analyzing successful experience in the market-place. The Ronald Series on Marketing Management is thus intended to communicate the state-of-the-art in marketing to managers.

Virtually all areas of marketing management will be explored in the series. Books now available or being planned cover advertising management, industrial, marketing research, brand loyalty, sales management, product policy and planning, public relations, overall marketing strategy, consumer behavior, and financial aspects of marketing management. It is hoped that the series will have some effect in raising the standards of applied marketing management.

FREDERICK E. WEBSTER, JR.

Hanover, New Hampshire

vii

Preface

Here is a book about consumer research that is an original and practical guide for tackling real-world business problems. It deals with specific cases of, and the methodology for, applied research into consumer behavior.

Substantive consumer research problems are the prime concern here. Techniques are introduced in a subordinate way, as a means to solving these problems. I also present problems and techniques that relate to actual practice.

This book provides only a limited treatment of multivariate techniques, emphasizing, instead, other statistical techniques—analysis of variance and bivariate and univariate significance tests—that have a greater variety of applications in the consumer research field.

Since this book deals with the application of consumer research to management decisions, I have emphasized quantitative rather than qualitative research. Qualitative research (focus groups, one-on-one depth interviews) is used to uncover variables and develop hypotheses. Quantitative research is used to identify problems and to aid in management decision making.

This book has been written specifically to meet the needs of those involved in consumer research. It will serve as an essential reference for marketing researchers in a variety of organizations—manufacturers, advertising agencies, advertising media, research companies, and so on. But it will be useful to anyone with a modicum of exposure to the basic ideas of consumer research, such as students who are focusing on marketing research, behavioral scientists, and managers who use consumer research in their decisions.

The primary objective of this book is to provide information, training, updating, and review so that important marketing problems can be solved effectively by consumer researchers. The book's secondary objective is to provide the reader with the tools to: (1) define marketing problems and opportunities, (2) consider alternative research designs that are efficient and sound, (3) analyze data to minimize risk in decision-making, and (4) interpret research results for more effective marketing.

This comprehensive and practical guide shows consumer researchers how to apply research methodology to their consumer research.

x   PREFACE

Twenty years ago, when I began my studies in consumer research, my efforts in this area were extensions of what I had learned about research methods from my mentors in the graduate sociology department at Columbia University. Over the years I came to realize that the field of consumer research is really a distinct discipline and I set out to codify and integrate this field. This book is the result of these endeavors.

I have written a state-of-the-art book that presents the best ways of doing research. The best ways of doing research are not necessarily the traditional ways.

I am deeply indebted to my wife Sheila for her research assistance, as well as for her insights, ideas, and invaluable comments. Thanks are due also to Douglas Banik, Karen Forcade, Jeff Harris, Elliott Lewis, Bob Prince, and Carole Prince for their kind assistance with various sections of the writing.

I wish to express my appreciation to the SAS Institute and to the Institute for Social Research of the University of Michigan for permission to illustrate computer solutions to examples using SAS and Osiris AID III, respectively.

MELVIN PRINCE

Greenwich, Connecticut
December, 1981

Contents

PART THREE   PRODUCT RESEARCH

PART FOUR   PROMOTION RESEARCH

EPILOGUE

PART ONE

GENERAL INTRODUCTION

ONE

Introduction

In the story dating from antiquity, a woman gave a man some fruit to eat. The fruit was taken from a tree in the middle of a garden.

THE DAWN OF CONSUMER RESEARCH

This was the world's first consumer research project and some of this project's results are common knowledge. But what details were left from this narrative as it was handed down by word of mouth?

Well, the woman in the story was the world's first consumer researcher. This woman's specialty was new products research. Her research approach was to present one respondent with one new product and wait for the response.

Many generations later, consumer research flourished. By then progress in consumer research included the use of fully clothed, trained interviewers. Research organizations became plentiful. One such company, Creation Research, Incorporated, of New Canaan had considerable experience in conducting sophisticated studies.

Creation Research's client, Forbidden Fruit, Incorporated, was interested in finding a good brand name for a new line of apples. Previous work in focus groups led to the selection of three names as most promising: Adam's Apples, Tree of Knowledge Apples, and Apples from Eden. A mail survey was sent to a sample of 6000 apple buyers.

A multistage sample was used. Names were taken randomly from town lists in Shinar, Chaldea, and Negev. One-third of the overall list was sent one of the three names atop a description and picture of the product. Respondents were instructed to answer the questionnaire only if they had bought apples in the past month.

Apple buyers were asked whether they would prefer to buy the product described or their current brand of apples. A chi-square (χ^2) test for independent samples showed that Apples from Eden was the strongest name. The line was so named and was eminently successful. Later, Creation Research conducted a telephone study that evaluated an advertising campaign for Apples from Eden. The research concluded that the campaign was effective. The campaign had achieved its objective: the brand had cultivated a favorable image as a natural food.

This ancient account conveys a general idea of the field of consumer research. As the introduction unfolds, the definition becomes much more precise.

CONSUMER RESEARCH TODAY

Have you as a researcher ever asked yourself, "What is consumer research, really?" I have, and I'd like to share my views with you. The task can be made easier if I first cover a few basic ideas, beginning with "research design."

Research design is a plan for a research project's methods and operations. It is a means to achieve research goals efficiently. In particular, consumer research designs specify a plan for measuring consumer response and consumer characteristics.

Now I illustrate some of the thinking that goes into the design of a consumer research project. Suppose management is interested in marketing a new coffee brand. Management is considering one of three claims for this product: rich tasting, mellow, or aromatic. You, the researcher, are asked for a research design to help select the best of these claims.

You realize that two of these claims, rich tasting and mellow, are related. Both promise better taste.

The research design you use in this case calls for exposing each respondent to one claim only. If all three claims were to be shown to each respondent, the two related claims would split the vote. This would bias the research in favor of the third claim that is unique.

Sound research design makes the study appropriate to the marketing problem. In addition, precision of research data is balanced against the value of the desired information.

A careful research design by itself is no guarantee of a successful study. Errors are likely to occur while a study is in progress—serious ones. This brings up another fundamental idea, "implementation."

Implementation is control over procedures when a study is in progress. It is a research task that reduces nonsampling error from data collection and management. For consumer research practice, it means seeing that (1) test items such as ads, packages, or products are received in the field on time in correct quantities and in the appropriate condition; (2) questionnaires are constructed to provide accurate information about consumer responses to products and communications; (3) interviewers thoroughly understand and properly execute sampling and interviewing instructions so that personal opinions of target consumers are represented; and (4) data management doesn't confound conclusions about the marketing problem.

The role that implementation plays can be seen from the following example. A coffee manufacturer wants to test two different packages. The research design you use calls for a trial of the product at a central location test kitchen. Respondents are asked for their opinions about the product. The same product is used throughout the study. One group is assigned package M and another group package N. Therefore, differences in product ratings should reflect packaging effects.

You are now involved in the study's implementation and urged to complete the fieldwork as soon as possible. Timing would be shortened if each interviewer made use of one package. However, you insist that each interviewer test half of his or her respondents on each package in a random sequence. Yes, the study would have been completed faster with one package assigned to each interviewer. But you know your decision is right: *your* interviewer assignments lessen the chance of interviewer bias in your study.

Good implementation guides a study so that it conforms to its explicit design. When this design fails to anticipate a difficulty, special unbiased procedures for data collection and management must be improvised and implemented.

Design and implementation of research result in a data base for marketing intelligence. This brings up the last basic idea, "data analysis."

Data analysis is the mining of a study's data base for its meaning and value. It is a process by which you, the researcher, consider evidence, draw conclusions, and make recommendations. Data analysis as a consumer research activity typically involves the following: (1) the basic distributions are examined; (2) data are explored, and marketing hypotheses are tested by means of summary statistics, statistics of relationships, and statistical significance tests; (3) the main practical conclusions and recommendations are arrived at. These are keyed to results that relate to the most strategic marketing variables; and (4) remaining results are combed for further insights and qualifications relevant to marketing decisions.

The following discussion shows the kind of logic that underlies data analysis. The client wants to update the creative strategy for the company's coffee brand. You, the researcher, confer with the advertising agency's account executive over necessary information for this update. You recommend and design an attitude and usage study for the coffee market. One objective of this study is to determine the most important characteristics that motivate coffee buying. This information is to be used to help select creative themes for advertising the coffee brand.

The data you use are obtained from a study of coffee buyers. Information is collected on coffee brand buying purchase frequency and perceptions of brands in the market, including respondents' regular brands of coffee. To answer the question of importance ratings, you decide to analyze the data indirectly. Statistical work is done to show how other brands differ in perception from the respondents' regular brands. Characteristics that are seen as unique to the regular brand provide a useful clue to the importance of specific product characteristics.

Systematic data analysis makes a study's information coherent. Also, data analysis provides a check on the reliability of conclusions.

In the light of all this it is very tempting to say I have given you my views on the question "What is consumer research, really?" But at this point, let us summarize what has been said with a formal definition of consumer research.

Consumer research is the design, implementation, and analysis of research on consumer behavior for use in management decision making. Now, let's move on.

A description of this book's aims and its coverage provides additional understanding of the field.

A LOOK AT THIS BOOK

This section describes the book's features and provides suggestions to help you, the researcher, make best use of the materials.

Features of this book

Chapter 2 gives the rationale for a research design's contribution in "bottom line" terms, thus providing the basic theme that underlies the rest of the book. The book is organized by three broad classes of consumer research: (1) marketing strategy research, (2) product research, and (3) promotion research (see Exhibit 1.1).

Marketing strategy research is discussed in Chapters 3 and 4. These chapters show how consumer research is used to measure needs, perceptions, and preferences in product categories of interest. These consumer dispositions suggest problems in areas of product or promotion research. Chapters 5–7 deal with product research: tests of product ideas and actual products and their packages. Information about product strengths ties to promotion research efforts. Chapters 8 and 9 present information about promotion research. Advertising pretests and marketing campaign evaluations are discussed. Chapter 10 ties the discussion of problems together. It focuses on research programs—interrelated efforts to solve several problems for a single brand.

Which of these chapters should you consult for your next project? There is no simple answer. The kind and timing of research for a brand depends on several factors. These include product life cycle, sales volume, sales trend, market dominance, and prior research.

This book contains materials that meet the needs of researchers at all levels of responsibility in every type of organization in which consumer research is used.

The variety of consumer research problems presented is reasonably comprehensive. An informal poll of professionals suggests that the problems covered represent more than 90% of those actually encountered.

Specific features of this book include research cases (model reports) that

EXHIBIT 1.1   Framework to classify and interrelate consumer research problems.

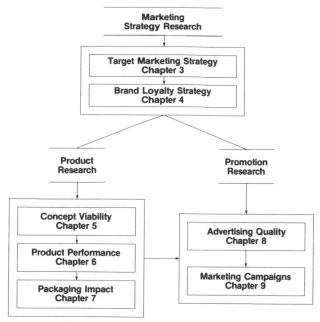

illustrate solutions to specific marketing problems. I have chosen to present research reports as cases. This has been done to simulate actual experience in research. The cases display the practical nature of consumer research and how technical principles are brought into play as a unity to serve the researcher's purpose.

Each case covers a different problem and a special design and uses a distinct statistical procedure. The inexperienced researcher is cautioned not to believe that there is one, and only one, simple solution to a given type of problem. For every consumer research problem, multiple solutions and a variety of research techniques could be applied. Then, based on the context in which the problem occurs, it is crucial to select the technique that fits best. There is more on this topic in the next chapter.

The objective of making this book practical for researchers has been served by elaborating on technical issues that arise in chapter cases. Technical appendices that are found after chapter summaries explain the analytical techniques used in the cases. Part II of the book shows applications of multivariate techniques. Parts III and IV deal with experimental design and bivariate techniques, respectively. Thus, although the high-powered statistical procedures are shown to have wide applicability in consumer research, other more commonly used, simpler procedures have not been ignored. Chapter-by-chapter coverage of specific analytic techniques is given in Appendix A. Outside readings on these techniques are found in Appendix B.

How to Use This Book

Emphasize in your reading what's important to you in your job. It isn't absolutely necessary that you read the book in detail, from cover to cover. For example, if you work for an advertising agency, you may want to concentrate your reading on chapters covering advertising quality and marketing campaigns. If you are a beginner, don't worry about the Technical Appendix sections; these sections can be omitted. You may want to consult the sections later, as the need arises, in your work.

Both beginners and more-advanced researchers can profit by a careful reading of the research cases that can provide an understanding of how to do the following:

Specify the research problem.
Decide what critical information is needed.
Define the sample that relates to the problem.
Select appropriate data collection techniques.
Search for analytical tools for assessing results.
Evaluate the marketing implications of research data.

Cases of exploratory studies of consumers' natural behavior are most instructive. Uncontrolled and nonexperimental field studies probe the full range of consumer research problems. Understanding the logic of exploratory studies is key for a grasp of the field as a whole.

SUMMARY

In this introductory chapter, *consumer research* is defined as the design, implementation, and analysis of research on consumer behavior for use in management decision making.

The book's basic theme is the value that consumer research design contributes to the decision-making process. The approach used to develop this theme is to present cases to simulate actual experience in research. This approach displays the practical nature of the field.

TWO
Research Design

A general understanding of research design is essential for solving any research problems faced. Chapter 1 briefly introduced the basic idea of research design. I defined research design as a plan for a research project's methods and operations. Now, I elaborate on this definition.

Research design is a plan that covers four general areas:

Sampling.
Access to the sampling unit.
Measurement.
Interpretation guidelines.

To illustrate, a research design for a coffee brand may call for information from the sample that can be generalized to all U.S. consumers (sampling), with data collected by central location telephone interviews (access to the sampling unit), to obtain perceptions and ratings of selected coffee brands (measurement) used to discover important coffee market segments (interpretation).

That is the overview. When you plan a complete research project, you must analyze the general areas of research design in detail. The purpose of this chapter is to show you how that is done and how it leads to the best research design.

PROBLEMS OF RESEARCH DESIGN

The most difficult—but rewarding—task you face is the design of consumer research. Consider, again, the coffee brand example. The study objective in this case is to provide data for selection of an advertising strategy. The full research design for the study must answer these—and other—questions: Whom should you interview? Where should the interview take place? Which brands should you talk about? What kinds of things should you show the consumer? How many different ways should the main study brand be shown to one respondent? What routines do you want the respondent to undergo? What questions do you want answered? How should these questions be asked? In what order should the questions be asked? How should responses be recorded? How much information do you need? And, when you're all done, what does the research information really mean?

This section outlines and simplifies the basic choices you make in selecting research designs. The section shows how to select alternative designs for any consumer research problem.

Each choice in research design is appropriate in some situations. You should master the basic principles covered. These principles tell you *when* the choice is appropriate. With better choices, the research designs you select will lead to more reliable management decisions.

Exhibit 2.1 is a checklist of critical issues in research design. The list is a handy means for you to classify designs. It is a tool for relating design elements to the research objectives. However, it is an imperfect tool. No list will guarantee you, the researcher, an error-free investigation. Use the list to plan for less-than-perfect information that will lead to the right decisions.

Examine the various items in Exhibit 2.1. These items apply to the research cases in subsequent chapters. The insights you have into these cases will be enriched by your understanding the choices underlying research design.

Unit of Analysis

The discussion begins by considering choices faced by you, the researcher, when the study sample is defined. The category user is likely to be the sample

EXHIBIT 2.1   Some Basic Choices in Consumer Research Design

Design Items	Some Basic Choices
Unit of analysis	Category user Category purchaser Company brand user Company brand purchaser
Data collection method	Personal Telephone Mail
Stimulus presentation	Brand unidentified Brand identified
Consumer response	Monadic Repeat
Evaluation criteria	Competitor brand(s) Company brand

for attitude and usage studies of the market for the product type. Category purchasers are a frequent unit of analysis for market segmentation studies. When a product is being reformulated, company brand users are the usual respondents. Company brand purchasers are typically the sample when repositioning is in progress and promotional efforts are evaluated.

Data Collection Method

The initial choice of personal contact, telephone, or mail as the mode of data collection should be based on the following:

Sampling accuracy.

Information requirements.

Administration of the instruments.

Quality of response.

Timing.

Cost considerations are discussed later as part of the overall research design. The pros and cons of three basic data collection methods are shown in Exhibit 2.2.

The personal interview is frequently used to do product research. This kind of research is often experimental, requiring complex tasks and tightly controlled administration of stimuli. In the product performance tests, the telephone may be used to follow up after the product is placed personally or by mail. The telephone is very useful for studies of marketing campaigns. It can provide representative samples, quick results, and precision timing when results are time dependent.

Stimulus Presentation

The choice of presenting a stimulus as a brand unidentified (i.e., "blind") is an important issue faced in product concept viability and product performance research.

At times, you will test product concepts without brand name labels. There are several reasons for this: (1) Management may want to know the interest level in the concept itself. Introduction of a brand name might confuse results. (2) Several names will be tested in a later research stage. The concept must first qualify itself in a consumer test. (3) The concept may be an entry that opens an entirely new market. The entry's name in such a case could be a minor issue at the outset.

Sometimes, products are unidentified by brand when given to consumers for testing. These blind product tests remove brand name influences that may hide underlying product qualities of interest.

At other times, product research is designed to identify the brands of the

EXHIBIT 2.2 Some Pros and Cons of Data Collection Methods

	Personal		Telephone		Mail	
	Pros	Cons	Pros	Cons	Pros	Cons
Sampling Accuracy	Easiest to develop representative samples Best for completion rates	Usually necessary to cluster interviews for cost efficiency Intercept studies subject to bias in respondent selection	Cost efficient not to cluster interviewing by area	Limited to telephone owner households	Cost efficient not to cluster interviews by area Easy to obtain sample dispersion	Nonpanel surveys result in greater nonresponse If panel, limited to those who agree to panel membership Information may come from other household members
Information Requirements	Best for obtaining large amounts of information if done in respondent's home	Intercept interviews may be hurried and dilute information quality	Intermediate amount of information when calls are made at convenient times	More difficult to obtain unstructured information Limited use for collecting complex data	Interview not rushed and can reflect thoughtful report	Variable amount of information, depending on topic and the amount of respondent effort required Limited use for collection of complex data Not appropriate for questions that need spontaneous response

Administration of Instrument	Can present visual materials Good for presentation of experimental tasks	Interviewer cheating problems	Central location validation highly accurate through monitoring Better controls over interviewer performance	Visual materials cannot be presented	No briefing of interviewers required	Lack of control over who actually answers questionnaire
Quality of Response	Better response available because of exposure to higher-quality stimuli	Strong potential for bias because of interviewer	Best for obtaining reliable, spontaneous responses to standardized questions and phrasing	Moderate potential for bias because of interviewer effect	Anonymity helps to assure accuracy for sensitive topics	Potential for error because of respondent confusion
Timing	Relatively fast way to collect data	Weather conditions can cause difficulty and delay	Fastest way to collect data	Capacity overload problems can cause delays	Relative timing improves when mail is used for samples difficult to access	Slowest way to collect data

13

products placed. The aim of such research is to learn how both the brand name and product affect consumer attitudes. For other kinds of consumer research problems, brands are invariably identified.

Consumer Response

A research design is monadic when only one stimulus is presented to each respondent. In contrast, there is the repeat measures design. Repeat measures are classed into sequential monadic and side by side. Sequential designs are monadic, staggered in time. Side-by-side tests invite direct comparisons of alternatives presented together.

Choices you, the researcher, make in consumer response between monadic and repeat options relate to (1) validity, (2) reliability, (3) sensitivity, and (4) feasibility.

1.   Let's begin with the validity issue. Monadic tests are valid in that consumers actually often use one brand exclusively over an extended period of time. Yet, unlike monadic designs, repeat measures provide a critical frame of reference in the respondent's mind. With repeat measures, you aim to control conditions found in monadic tests, such as "novelty effects."

2.   The reliability of monadic versus repeat measure studies depends on the individual case. Repeat studies are less reliable when previous responses contaminate a measurement. In such cases, you may find product attributes under- or overrated and their importance unduly exaggerated.

Monadic studies are less reliable when there are serious between-group differences in variables unrelated to the study. For example, study conditions may differ between groups. These differences may produce unreliable results and conclusions.

3.   Sometimes guidance is needed for a choice between alternatives. In such cases, repeat measures give greater assurance that the research will provide the required sensitivity. Repeat measures must be used when you test minor variations, for example, color or scent.

4.   Finally, the decision you make between monadic and repeat consumer response often hinges on the option's feasibility. For example, respondents may be unwilling to use test products for more than a one-month period. This might eliminate the sequential use of products for studies calling for longer use periods.

Evaluation Criteria

The basic issue in setting evaluation criteria is the selection of an appropriate control for interpretation. Because of research costs, you may be faced with a choice of control between competitor brands and the company brand. Once this choice is made, you can develop evaluation criteria to include (1) measures to be used for interpretation and (2) decision rules for interpretation of comparisons with the control.

For existing brands, how do you choose between competitor brands and the company brand as the control? The answer depends on the inferences you can make about marketplace performance under a given alternative. Suppose, for example, a product substitution is considered. The research shows that differences between the new and current product are undetectable to consumers. It is reasonable for you to infer in this case that the changeover will not affect the brand's marketplace performance.

When the research deals with new products, you will likely use the company brand as the control. This is especially true when the company dominates the market with existing brands. With market dominance, the company runs less risk by employing its own brand as the control. An exception is the category's being a new venture for the company. In that case, it is obvious that use of competitive controls is indicated for the research.

When you consider it essential to use competitive controls, the problem branches even further. The critical choice then becomes which specific competitors do you select for the research? Select as controls those brands that are serious and direct competitors. These competitive brands may compete in the same price tiers, distribution channels, demographic, life-style, or product benefit segments.

The overall research design affects the basic choices for design items. Each choice in the research design relates to those for other items in the overall design. There is no specific sequence for making these basic choices.

The purpose of these choices is to create a detailed, integrated blueprint of procedures so that you can solve consumer research problems. This blueprint of procedures covers the units to be sampled and the information to be obtained. Marketing strategy, product, and promotion research have different information needs. Information obtained in these studies is shown in Exhibit 2.3

For any cost level it is possible to "tighten" a design to increase its accuracy. You must take care in the design to minimize slippages between the original problem and the plan, the plan and the plan's execution, and the plan's execution and the respondent's reactions.

An appropriate research design is this:

Sufficiently useful to solve the problem that prompts the request.

Characterized by a reasonable accuracy level.

Justifiable in costs and timing.

Feasible, with a reasonable chance of succeeding.

The task you have is to select and recommend the most appropriate of these alternative research designs.

EXHIBIT 2.3   Selected Areas of Measurement for Three Classes of Consumer Research

Marketing Strategy Research	Product Research	Promotion Research
Consumer needs	Product differentiation	Awareness
Ratings of importance of different product attributes	Expectations	Recall
	Preferences	Recognition
Perceptions and evaluations of competitive brands	Motivations	Comprehension
	Attribute ratings	Motivation
Purchase behavior	Aesthetics	Meaning
Demographic characteristics	Purchase behavior	Preference
	Demographic characteristics	Purchase behavior
		Demographic characteristics

SELECTION OF THE BEST DESIGN

A design for consumer research must reduce the costs of wrong decisions. The value of the design you select is the amount of positive difference between the value of the information it provides and the costs of obtaining that information. The best design is not necessarily the most accurate one. *The best design has the greatest value.* It is the design you select to best allocate available research dollars.

It is possible for you to formalize and quantify judgments that underlie decisions about research designs. Quantified judgments become values used for computations, based on statistical decision theory, for selection of the best design. The theory is exact, but the judgments are somewhat error prone. The usefulness of the decision theory approach depends on the reliability of judgments about (1) payoffs relating to actions and marketplace outcomes, (2) the personal probabilities of the payoffs, (3) the accuracy level of the research design, and (4) the costs of the research, including the costs of the delay of marketplace action while the research is in progress.

To estimate a research design's value, you must make these computations:

Expected value of the design's payoff (the sum of the payoffs times their probabilities).

Expected net payoff for the design (difference between the payoff with the research information and the payoff without such information).

Value of the design (expected net payoff, minus research costs, including the costs of the delay).

You now have the concepts and procedures for the use of statistical decision theory to select the best research design. Use of the theory is illustrated by means of a case.

A RESEARCH DESIGN CASE

Robertson coffee's market share dropped from 30 to 21% within one year. The giant, nationally distributed brand clearly was in trouble.

In an effort to improve sales, management experimented with a package change. The purpose of this package change was to improve shelf life and product freshness.

However, a test market study showed that a change to a new package would only aggravate the sales problems Robertson coffee was having. The test market saved management from making a costly error.

A management committee reviewed the situation. It was decided that the problem most likely stemmed from Robertson's current advertising strategy. The advertising agency was informed of this conclusion.

In response, the account management supervisor of the agency suggested an attitude and usage study. By segmenting the market, this study was to help develop strategy for a new campaign. The client's advertising management expressed interest in the idea. The client requested a research proposal.

Agency researchers designed a study to meet the objective. This study would be conducted by telephone among a nationally projectible telephone household sample of 2000 coffee buyers. It would cost $90,000 and take about eight to nine weeks to complete. After several agency-client meetings, the client raised a critical question. Wouldn't it be better to use the information available from past research instead of doing the new study? (The information dated from the time the brand was only in regional distribution—seven years ago.) This would eliminate costly delays in starting the new advertising campaign and would save the proposed research expenditure of $90,000.

The agency research director was asked to work on this problem. He quickly reviewed current coffee market data from outside sources. Then the current coffee market data were compared with the information from past research. The comparison showed that the past data were clearly obsolete. It was agreed to consider the old information as no information.

Then based on discussions between the client and the agency, the agency research director developed a payoff table of values for several marketing alternatives. The analysis revealed that the value of information from the proposed research would exceed the estimated research cost. Therefore, the client agreed to proceed with the research. However, another question was raised. The client felt that personal interviews would provide high-quality information from respondents relative to telephone interviews.

Wouldn't it be better to spend the same $90,000 on personal interviews and complete the study in the same time frame?

The account management supervisor was prepared for this question. He argued that information collected by telephone leads to higher payoffs, given equal costs. For a fixed cost, many more telephone interviews than personal interviews could be completed. In addition, a telephone probability sample would be more representative than multimarket, personal intercept interviews. Finally, the cost of door-to-door personal interviews for a national probability sample was totally prohibitive for the problem.

Convinced, the client agreed to proceed with the agency's study as originally proposed. The study's objective was to help develop a new ad campaign, that is, provide information to determine (1) copy strategy and (2) media mix. To achieve this objective, the design called for an attitude and usage study among a national telephone probability sample of 2000 consumers who had bought coffee in the past month.

A researcher supplier was called in to provide cost and timing estimates. To help make these estimates, the supplier was told that (1) coffee buyers are 60% of the adult population and (2) the average interview length would be one-half hour (about 60 questions).

Areas of measurement included the following:

Attitudes toward coffee in general.
Attitudes toward types or varieties of coffee.
   Sizes.
   Forms.
   Packaging.
Brand awareness.
Brand usage.
Reason for brand selection.
Consumption patterns.
   Frequency of use.
   Occasion of use.
Brand loyalty.
Size loyalty.
Coffee type loyalty.
Attributes desired in an ideal coffee brand.
Brand images.
   Suitability for specified occasions.
   User image profile.
   Price.
   Quality.
Psychographic characteristics.
   Independents.
   Economy minded.
   Tastemakers.

Traditionalists.
Indifferents.
Demographic characteristics.
Sex.
Age.
Income.
Education.

Data analysis called for segmentation of the coffee market by psychographic characteristics of coffee buyers. The research was designed to segment over 90% of coffee buyers into their appropriate consumer categories.

The client's research director was very interested in the method used to select the best design for this study and requested a presentation from the agency on this topic. Table 2.1 is a slide from that presentation. The agency research director explained this slide as follows:

At the top you see the three alternatives which were evaluated for the Robertson coffee research. A-1, telephone interviews with 2000 coffee buyers; A-2, personal interviews with 1500 coffee buyers; and A-3, act with no information.

TABLE 2.1   Selection of Best Research Design for Survey of the Coffee Market

Results	A-1 Telephone Interviews, 2000 Coffee Buyers	A-2 Personal Interviews, 1500 Coffee Buyers	A-3 Act with No Information
Probabilities			
Good campaign	.80	.80	.70
Bad campaign	.20	.20	.30
Payoffs (annual)			
Good campaign	3,500,000	3,250,000	3,000,000
Bad campaign	[1,250,000]*	[1,350,000]	[1,500,000]
Expected value of payoffs	2,550,000	2,330,000	1,650,000
Expected net payoff	900,000	680,000	—
Estimated cost of delay	275,000	275,000	—
Value of information	625,000	405,000	
Estimated research cost	90,000	90,000	
Value of design	$535,000	$315,000	

*[ ] indicates loss.

These were the options your management wanted us to look at. So, together with my account management supervisor, we had an all-night, tense, shirt-sleeve session with your ad manager.

To help us estimate what might happen, we looked at past advertising campaigns for several of our coffee brands, including Robertson's. We found that changes in campaigns, without the use of research, improved sales; but research-based campaigns were even more likely to work. Interestingly, the better the quality of the research, the more the campaign appeared to return in sales. The differences between all these new campaigns, however, was not very large. These clues helped us to agree on the personal probabilities and estimated payoffs for Robertson in the present situation.

Finally, we reached agreement on specific values for the probabilities of a good or bad campaign for Robertson's coffee, depending on the alternative considered. For example, A-2, use of personal interviews, was felt to provide information with an 80% chance of producing a good campaign. We also reached agreement on payoffs. Payoffs in this chart are an estimate of dollar profit, given either a good or bad campaign. For A-2, for example, a good campaign is presented as likely to have a payoff of $3,250,000 over a year. A bad campaign is given a negative payoff—unreturned advertising dollars.

The next row, the expected value of payoffs, is the result of multiplying corresponding probabilities and payoffs, then summing the products. For A-2, it's .80 × 3,250,000 minus .2 × 1,350,000. That's $2,330,000. The next row, expected net payoff, is simply the difference between a research design and A-3, act with no information, on expected value of payoffs. The cost of delay is estimated by multiplying the time required for a research project (8.66 weeks) by the expected value of payoffs for A-3, prorated for the same amount of time. That is $1,650,000 divided by 52, which is then multiplied by 8.66. The value of the information is the difference between the expected net payoff and the estimated cost of delay. For A-2, this is $680,000 less $275,000, or $405,000. The value of the design is the value of information less the estimated research cost. For A-2, the value of the design is $315,000—a good design. However, alternative A-1 is the best design for the Robertson coffee research, with a value of $535,000.

This is what I'd like to leave you with. [See Table 2.2.]

This table provides relative cost information for study designs using different data collection techniques. It will help you greatly the next time you specify and evaluate alternative research designs.

SUMMARY

A *research design* is a plan that covers (1) sampling, (2) access to the sampling unit, (3) measurement, and (4) interpretation guidelines.

A design can be quite complex in its full detail. The object is to simplify the procedures by making the basic choices first. These choices relate to the following:

Unit of analysis.

Data collection method.

Stimulus presentation.

Consumer response.

Evaluation criteria.

The overall research design affects the basic research choices. The result is an integrated design, appropriate for the problem.

The best design can be selected from alternatives by application of statistical decision theory. The best design provides the highest return on the investment in research.

Research must be custom designed for each project you do. There are no simple formulas. Designs vary by a brand's dominance and profitability and the risk in the marketing alternatives of the problem. In the cases that follow, each research design reflects the unique challenge faced by the researcher.

TABLE 2.2   Cost per Interview of Data Collection for Consumer Research (Indexed)[a]

	Incidence Rate						
	100%	80%	60%	40%	20%	10%	5%
Twenty questions[b]							
Mail	1.00	1.25	1.67	2.50	5.00	10.00	20.00
Telephone	1.28	1.54	1.85	2.18	3.04	4.78	8.25
Personal	1.39	1.58	1.81	2.04	2.69	4.00	6.60
Forty questions							
Mail	1.04	1.30	1.74	2.61	5.22	10.40	20.88
Telephone	2.52	2.76	3.06	3.39	4.37	6.00	9.48
Personal	2.69	2.89	3.02	3.35	4.00	5.30	7.90
Sixty questions							
Mail	1.46	1.82	2.43	3.64	7.29	14.59	29.17
Telephone	3.82	4.06	4.37	4.37	5.56	7.30	10.77
Personal	4.00	4.19	4.41	4.65	5.30	6.60	9.22

[a]The table is read in the following way: The cost of an interview is located by selecting the incidence rate for the target group studied, the number of structured questions, and the data collection method, that is, by mail, telephone, or personal. Questions assumed to be closed-end, rather than free-response for approximating costs.
[b]Mail based on contact with mail panel. Telephone for central location calls only. Personal for central location only.

PART TWO

MARKETING STRATEGY RESEARCH

THREE
Target Market Strategy

The target market is the prospect group selected for marketing emphasis. Management wants a description of the target market: the brand's present and potential consumers. The challenge for you is to locate these consumers so that targeted communications can be highly efficient. Shifts in consumer values and market entries mean that brand prospects must be redefined as new classes of consumers.

Chapter 2 showed ways of handling basic choices in the design of research for any problem. In this chapter I cover the first of a series of specific consumer research problems—target market strategy studies. These studies do more than identify the target consumer for a brand. They also explore consumers' perceptions, needs, and behavior.

Through target market strategy studies, you explore market segments of interest to a company. Let's see what you, the researcher, do to bring marketing problems to light—to help a company strengthen its target market strategy.

Shape creative, media, and promotional strategies. With target market strategy information, management examines the efficiency of past and ongoing marketing activities. Alternative strategies are weighed, leading to specific decisions for marketing a brand.

Using target market strategy information, these decisions cover the following:

Creative Strategy. How to appeal to underdeveloped segments, exploit the brand's image, and use presenters in commercials who are believable and persuasive.

Media Strategy. How to provide for extra effort in targeting to more valuable and responsive groups and set guidelines for an appropriate media mix.

Promotional strategy. How to develop themes for promotions that will appeal to target groups.

Based on target market strategy research, management estimates what will happen if various strategies are acted on. With these estimates in mind, an agenda is set for a brand.

Describe customers for market or a brand. In your studies, you describe a market's customers and their needs and expectations. Management wants to know what important benefits consumers think brands in the market offer or fail to offer. Which brands define the market, for the purpose of study, depends on how well stratified the market is—that is, whether customers limit their choices to certain types of brands. For example, a strategy study for a manufacturer of a quality piano might measure only prestige name, high priced pianos. The assumption in this study would be that the piano market is highly stratified by brand reputation and price.

Target market strategy studies look at market opportunities for a specific brand. Research informs management of the chief ways its brand's competitive position can be improved.

You shape strategies and describe customers by doing different types of target market strategy studies. Exhibit 3.1 shows specific problems encountered in target market strategy research. Each of the problems concerns the total market and is classified by whether the primary measurement is consumer activities or attitudes. Let's examine these research problems.

IDENTIFYING PROSPECTS FOR A BRAND

Target market strategy research must define a brand's prospects to help strengthen that brand's marketing mix. Defining the prospects for a brand means identifying, evaluating, and selecting a set of consumers who are predisposed to try the brand and to be satisfied.

Brand prospect studies classify and describe the target market in several ways. These studies deal with demographic descriptions (sex, marital status, education, age, geographics), "sociographics" (life-style variables such as leisure activities, value system), and "psychographics" (such as personality descriptions).

Once you identify and describe the target market, you can estimate its size by projecting from the target market sample to the target market population. Conversion rates are applied to target market estimates to determine if the group of consumers actually using the product is large enough to provide a profitable return. A major advantage of understanding the target market is that

EXHIBIT 3.1   Examples of Target Market Strategy Problems

Research Problem	Study Sample	Primary Measurement
Identifying prospects for a brand	Total market	Consumer activity
Creating brand impressions	Total market	Consumer attitude

you can make specific recommendations on where to spend advertising dollars, that is, in selection of media for carrying advertising.

Case Preview: "Instant Curls" Electric Hairstylers

Case 3.1, Instant Curls, illustrates the role marketing strategy research can play in defining the market for a brand. Also, it shows how target market data are used to build a media schedule for advertising a new product in an existing product category. The success of Instant Curls depended on identifying, evaluating, and satisfying the important consumer segments, since there were so many women using electric hairstylers, with varying needs and wants for this product. These segments were sizable groups of consumers, expected to be most responsive to this brand's special benefits. No other electric hairstyler could match Instant Curls on the speed of forming curls.

The company introducing Instant Curls had a line of home appliances used primarily by women. As a starting point, company files were ransacked for available statistics on women who use appliances. The search failed to uncover recent, useful data. This particular target market study then was requested by brand management at a meeting with marketing research. The brand manager explained the need for target market data to develop a sound media schedule for advertising Instant Curls. The market researcher suggested a sophisticated design for describing the market segments toward which the advertising would be geared. He used a research plan that included measurements of demographic and sociographic variables, as well as usual electric hairstyler use. The heavy user was felt to be a better brand prospect for Instant Curls. However, the brand manager wanted to limit the study to demographics: he wanted something "quick, dirty, and inexpensive." At marketing's request, the researcher revised his design to cover the same demographics used in previous studies. The information was an accurate update of high-priority information that satisfied marketing and research.

According to a clustering technique called "Automatic Interaction Detector" (AID) analysis, the market for this product was women under 50, with incomes under $25,000 who were living in the non-West. Having this information made it simple for the researcher to project to the U.S. population and estimate the size of the target market. With pricing and other information supplied by marketing management, the researcher determined that this was a large enough marketing segment for concentrating marketing effort on Instant Curls.

Case 3.1   Segmentation of Purchasers of "Instant Curls" Electric Hairstylers

Objective

An appliance company markets Instant Curls, the leading brand of electric hairstylers. The objective of this study is to describe demographically the target market for this product, so as to sharpen media planning.

Method

The data were collected by means of a national mail survey. This survey was conducted among 5000 women, 18 and older. Women 18 and older represent over nine-tenths of purchasers in the product category. The survey is based on 4430 completed usable questionnaires. This information is intended to be suggestive rather than strictly representative of the character of the target market. An AID analysis was used to identify key demographic segments. The target market in this study was defined as Instant Curls purchasers.

Recommendations and Conclusions

Based on the AID analysis, the primary target group for Instant Curls is comprised of women under 50. This segment is large in absolute terms (73.4% of women 18 and older) and has an incidence of use of 28.8%. Among women 50 and over, the percentage using Instant Curls is only 13.1%. The marketing effort against women 50 and over has been as strong as the effort against younger women. It appears that women 50 and over are far less responsive to the promotion of this product.

Segments combining several demographic variables were identified for more precise targeting. They are shown next, in order of size of customer group for Instant Curls:

Rank of Segment Size	Segment	Percentage of Population	Percentage of "Instant Curls" Purchasers in Population Segment
1	Under 50; under $25,000; non-West	43.6	21.6
2	Under 50; $25,000 and over; non-West	11.9	34.3
3	Under 50; under $25,000; West	12.9	29.8
4	Under 50; $25,000 and over; West	5.0	44.2
5	50 and over; under $25,000	18.4	9.8
6	50 and over; $25,000 and over; employed	3.6	21.4
7	50 and over; $25,000 and over; unemployed	4.6	11.3

It is recommended that media schedules for Instant Curl provide extra effort towards population segments with the highest percentages of Instant Curls purchasers. The resulting efficiencies should be expected to improve overall brand profit (see Tables 1 and 2).

The incidence of purchasing Instant Curls electric hairstylers varies directly with income: that is, with higher income, the proportion buying the brand in

TABLE 1   Demographic Segments in AID Analysis that Maximize Differences in the Percentage of "Instant Curls" Purchases

AID Segment	Percentage Purchasing Instant Curl
Total sample	22.2
$25,000 and over versus	29.3
Under $25,000	19.0
50 and over versus	13.1
Under 50	28.8
Employed versus	35.9
Unemployed	16.2
Rest of United States versus	19.4
West	27.7

TABLE 2   A.I.D. Tree for Segmentation of Instant Curl Purchasers.

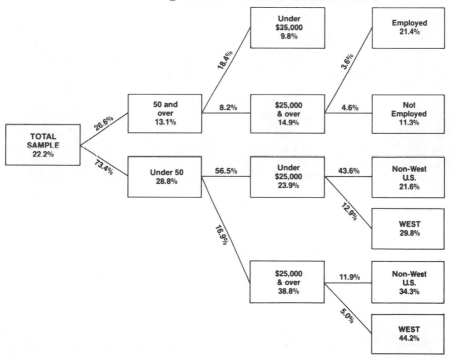

the past year increases from 14% among those with household incomes of $10,000 or under to 29% among those with household incomes of $25,000 and above (see Table 3).

The incidence of buying Instant Curls electric hairstylers is highest among respondents in the age group 35−49 (34%), followed by the under-35-year-old group (20%). It is lowest among older women, 13% for those 50 and over (see Table 4).

Women who are employed are more likely to have purchased an Instant Curls electric hairstyler in the past year than are women who are unemployed (see Table 5).

TABLE 3   "Instant Curls" Hairstylers Purchased in Past Year (by Household Income)

		Percentage			
Response	Total	Under $10,000	$10,000 − $14,999	$15,000 − $24,999	$25,000 and over
Yes	22	14	18	21	29
No	78	86	82	79	71
Base	(4430)	(560)	(840)	(1870)	(1160)

Question: Have you purchased any type of electric hairstyler in the past year? If yes, what brand did you purchase?

TABLE 4   "Instant Curls" Electric Hairstylers Purchased in Past Year (by Age)

		Percentage		
Response	Total	Under 35	35−49	50+
Yes	22	20	34	13
No	78	80	66	87
Base	(4430)	(1470)	(1670)	(1290)

Question: Have you purchased any type of electric hairstyler in the past year? If yes, what brand did you purchase?

TABLE 5   "Instant Curls" Electric Hairstylers Purchased in Past Year (by Employment)

		Percentage	
Response	Total	Unemployed	Employed
Yes	22	16	36
No	78	84	64
Base	(4430)	(1983)	(2447)

Question: Have you purchased any type of electric hairstyler in the past year? If yes, what brand did you purchase?

TABLE 6 "Instant Curls" Electric Hairstylers Purchased in Past Year (by Region)

Response	Total	North	East	South	West
	%	%	%	%	%
Yes	2	20	21	17	28
No	78	80	79	83	72
Base	(4430)	(912)	(1320)	(1098)	(1100)

Question: Have you purchased any type of electric hairstyler in the past year? If yes, what brand did you purchase?

Women who live in the West are more likely than women in other geographical locations to have purchased an Instant Curls hairstyler in the past year (see Table 6).

CREATING BRAND IMPRESSIONS

When you have identified brand prospects, you have only begun your job. The research you do also must deal with brand impressions to make this market receptive.

Brand image research involves uncovering variables relating to a brand's reputation and measuring them. The objective is to help find ways to create the most positive brand image so that consumers will favor your brand over all competitive brands.

Ideally, a product manager wants to create a brand image favorable to sales that helps (1) retain present customers, (2) capture brand switchers, and (3) attract new users to the product category.

Brand image studies establish what attributes are most important for differentiating, evaluating, and comparing brands in a product category. These attributes may include pricing, design, packaging, product performance, name and user imagery. When you compare attributes of a company's brand with those of an "ideal" product in the category and with attribute ratings of the other available brands, you are able to help brand management learn what about their brand helps or hinders its purchase. The closer a brand is rated to the ideal, the more likely it is to be a dominant brand in its category.

Case Preview: "Charge-Up" Nutrition Bar

Case 3.2, Charge-Up, illustrates a research response to a brand manager's often asked question: "What keeps nonusers of my brand from switching to this brand?" Charge-Up had been a leader in the nutrition bar category, but with the introduction of five new brands in the past two years and many new users entering this category, it had lost eight important share points. It was this company's most important brand. The company was very concerned with developing a strategy that would increasingly allow it to capture brand switchers. Based on this marketing objective, the problems the researchers faced were to determine Charge-Up's image among competitive brand users and describe their ideal product and obtain ratings of the strengths and weaknesses of their current brand.

The brand manager liked the research design because it tied closely to marketing objectives. Once this study was completed, he would be able to implement strategies for best exploiting Charge-Up's strengths and competitive products' weaknesses.

The perceived "beneficiality" of Charge-Up seemed to be a major source of purchase resistance, according to a predictive technique used, discriminant analysis. The scaled discriminant weight for beneficiality was stronger than for other sources of resistance studied. Based on this information, the advertising made use of a slogan: "Be good to yourself, eat 'Charge-Up,' " and placed more emphasis on Charge-Up's nutritional benefits in the sales message. Research and development began to examine the ingredients and clinical evidence to see if Charge-Up would be able to claim a competitive edge in nutritional benefits in its future advertising.

Case 3.2   Resistance to Purchase of "Charge-Up" Nutrition Bar

Objective

This study was conducted as part of an overall program for further expanding Charge-Up nutrition bar's franchise. The purpose of this research was to answer the question: "Why don't current nonusers of the brand purchase the brand?" To identify key advertising objectives, the research was organized to provide information to permit identification of basic sources of resistance and the effect on levels of company performance for each of these basic sources of purchase resistance.

Method

A total of 2000 adults, ages 35–50, not currently using Charge-Up were selected randomly from five geographically dispersed cities. Interviews were conducted by telephone. A discriminant function analysis was used to identify variables important for predicting resistance to brand use.

Recommendations and Conclusions

The discriminant function analysis disclosed that resistance to the purchase of Charge-Up was greatest when the product was thought to be less beneficial than other brands. This suggests that the primary thrust of advertising might be comparative, showing why Charge-Up does more than other brands for consumers' energy and nutritional needs.

The results of the discriminant analysis show that when identified sources of resistance are combined 74% of the resistant are classified correctly and 59% of the nonresistant. This indicates that the analysis provides a reasonable model of what is involved in resistance to the purchase of Charge-Up.

For the Charge-Up brand nonuser, predisposition to buy the brand depends heavily on promoting a favorable series of brand images (listed next). Advertising directed to achieve these objectives has the greatest potential for positively affecting the buying behavior of nonusers, ages 35–50.

Of seven basic sources of resistance having direct implications for creating advertising, five relate to brand image, two to advertising recall. They are as follows:

Brand Image
Beneficiality.
Value for the money.
Activity level of the brand user.
The brand's delivering on its promise of performance.
Price compared to other brands.

Advertising Recall
"Good for tired people."
"Helps maintain health."

Those who are the most inclined to purchase Charge-Up are more likely to perceive the brand as a product for the "active" than is the case for those less inclined to buy the product. A parity pricing image is the most favorable positioning for effecting purchase among nonusers (see Table 1).

To overcome purchase resistance, further improvement is needed in the following brand images: beneficiality, Charge-Up's delivering on its promise of performance, and value for the money. The optimal performance level for beneficiality is 59% (positively predisposed toward purchase), but only 30% of the entire sample rates the brand as either "very much more" or "somewhat more" beneficial, as compared to other brands (see Table 2).

Charge-Up's value for the money achieved either an "excellent" or "good" rating by 54% of the sample, considerably less than the optimal level of 75% among those already positively predisposed to purchase (see Table 3).

In terms of the brand's delivering on its promise of performance, the level achieved by the entire sample falls below the optimal level achieved by nonusers positively predisposed to purchase. On 10-point constant sum scale, 37% of all non-users rate the brand in the top 4 points, compared with 63% of the positively predisposed nonusers who rate the brand in the top 4 points. See Table 4.

TABLE 1   Why Women, Ages 35–50, Do Not Purchase "Charge-Up" Nutrition Bar Product.

Basic Sources of Purchase Resistance[a]		Scaled Discriminant Weight
Brand knowledge		
Brand image		
Less beneficial than other brands		.56
Poor value for money		.31
Lower activity level of brand A user		−.31
Charge-Up performance less than promised		.28
Not at parity with other brands on expensiveness		−.22
Advertising recall		
No recall of "Good for tired people"		−.22
No recall of "Helps maintain health"		.19
Profile characteristics		
Higher education		.18
Classification results		
Predicted	Resistant	Nonresistant
Actual		
Resistant	74	26
Nonresistant	41	59

[a]Included because a discriminant function analysis indicates these sources are basic for explaining purchase intent.

"Helps maintain health" achieves a satisfactory level of recall; "Good for tired people" achieves a less than satisfactory level. Although "Helps maintain health" achieves a satisfactory level of recall, "Good for tired people" is much further from the optimal level of recall. Among all nonusers, 37% recalls "Helps maintain health," compared to the optimal of 42% of nonusers already positively predisposed toward the purchase. "Good for tired people" is recalled by 66% of all nonusers, compared to the optimal 84% among nonusers positively predisposed. See Table 5.

Media Implications

The most responsive source of the brand's prospects among those 35–50 are nonusers who have not exceeded a high school education. Targeting to this segment should be most productive in today's market. See Table 6.

TABLE 2 Perceived Beneficiality of "Charge-Up" Compared to Other Brands (by Predisposition to Buy "Charge-Up")

Rating of "Charge-Up" in comparison to Other Brands	Percentage Predisposed to Buy "Charge-Up"			
	Total	Definitely or Probably Would Buy	Might or Might Not Buy	Probably Not or Definitely Not Buy
Very much more beneficial	9	20	3	3
Somewhat more beneficial	21	39	17	6
About the same	55	40	72	56
Somewhat less beneficial	8	1	5	17
Very much less beneficial	5	—	—	14
Don't know	2	—	3	4
Base	(197)	(69)	(64)	(64)

Question: Which one of the following statements best describes your opinion of Charge-Up in comparison to other brands, regardless of whether you have ever used Charge-Up?

TABLE 3 Perceived Value of "Charge-Up" (by Predisposition to Buy "Charge-Up")

"Charge-Up" Rating of in Terms of Value for the Money	Percentage Predisposed to Buy "Charge-Up"			
	Total	Definitely or Probably Would Buy	Might or Might Not Buy	Probably Would Not or Definitely Would Not Buy
Excellent value	7	14	3	2
Good value	47	61	52	27
Fair value	31	20	38	36
Poor value	9	—	2	27
Don't know	6	5	5	8
Base	(197)	(69)	(64)	(64)

Question: In terms of value for the money would you say that Charge-Up is an excellent value, good value, fair value or poor value?

TABLE 4 "Charge-Up" 's Promise of Performance (by Predisposition to Buy "Charge-Up")

Rating of "Charge-Up"[a]	Total	Percentage Predisposed to Buy "Charge-Up"		
		Definitely or Probably Would Buy	Might or Might Not Buy	Probably Would Not or Definitely Would Not Buy
10	12	20	11	5
9	4	7	3	2
8	12	22	9	5
7	9	14	8	5
6	9	6	11	11
5	36	26	45	38
4	2	1	2	3
3	2	—	2	5
2	3	—	2	8
1	6	—	5	16
Don't know	5	4	5	2
Base	(197)	(69)	(64)	(64)

Question: Some products may do everything they promise, while other products may make promises but do nothing. On a scale from 1 to 10, where 1 represents a product that does everything it promises, how would you rate a Charge-Up nutrition bar?

[a]Rating of 10: "Does everything it promises." Rating of 1: "Makes promises but does nothing."

TABLE 5 Aided Recall of "Charge-Up" Advertising (by Predisposition to Buy "Charge-Up")

Advertising Claims Recalled for "Charge-Up"	Total	Percentage Predisposed to Buy		
		Definitely or Probably Would Buy	Might or Might Not Buy	Probably Would Not or Definitely Would Not Buy
Helps maintain health	37	42	38	31
Good for tired people	66	84	57	56
Base	(191)	(67)	(63)	(61)

Question: Which of the following claims do you recall seeing or hearing for Charge-Up?

TABLE 6   Respondent's Education (by Predisposition to Buy "Charge-Up")

Last Grade of School Completed	Total	Percentage Predisposed to Buy "Charge-Up"		
		Definitely or Probably Would Buy	Might or Might Not Buy	Probably Would Not or Definitely Would Not Buy
Grade school or less	3	3	5	—
Some high school	16	23	13	11
Completed high school	41	54	38	31
Some college	24	14	26	33
Graduated college	16	6	18	25
Base	(197)	(69)	(64)	(64)

Question: What was the last grade of school you completed?

SUMMARY

Target market strategy research provides direction for strengthening a brand's position in the marketplace.

Target market strategy studies are used by decision makers in creative, media, and promotion areas. These decisions involve learning, through research, a brand's best image—and how to communicate it.

This type of behavior explores consumers' attitudes and behavior regarding a brand's product category. It identifies brand prospects and describes needs and expectations.

Before a brand image is created for a product, the target audience must be defined—that is, the group of consumers most likely to buy the brand. Once the target audience is defined, the appropriate brand image for target marketing can be developed.

Target market studies look broadly at markets. Other studies are designed to learn about a specific brand's consumer franchise. These studies describe brand use and purchase experience.

TECHNICAL APPENDIX

ALTERNATE DESIGNS FOR TARGET MARKET STRATEGY RESEARCH

Design Alternatives	Notes

Unit of analysis
  Category user
  Category purchaser
  Company brand user
  Company brand purchaser
	Special kinds of marketing strategy studies—such as segmentation and market mapping research—sample category purchasers and users.

Data collection method
  Personal
  Telephone
  Mail
	Complex analysis and projectible samples required. High incidence permits consideration of each data collection method.

Stimulus presentation
  Brand unidentified
  Brand identified
	Sometimes identified packaging or advertising is exposed as part of a wide-ranging inquiry.

Consumer response
  Monadic
  Repeat
	Repeat measures obtained—measures for each of a set of competitive brands.

Evaluation criteria
  Competitor brands
  Company brand
	When there is a company entry, evaluation includes both company and competitor brands.

ANALYTICAL TECHNIQUES

Techniques used in this chapter's target market strategy research cases are presented in this section. The specific techniques are Automatic Interaction Detector (AID) and discriminant analyses. These are classified under the general head of multivariate analyses.

Multivariate analyses involve three or more variables as a system. Basically, these techniques are extensions of simpler, statistical procedures on one or two variables.

AID and discriminant analyses are classified as predictive methods (estimating some variables from others). For multivariate predictive methods there are no restrictions on the number of independent or dependent variables allowed. Predictive multivariate techniques can improve marketing decisions when research results are based on a single, dependent variable.

AID

AID analyzes a total quantity by dividing it into amounts contributed by subgroups of respondents. The groups identified can be described by several variables, for example, young housewives living in the North and East. The analysis begins with a dependent variable, such as average purchase volume. The AID program will examine all possible splits of market segments so that the segments are homogeneous in themselves but differ between each other. A particular sex and age grouping, for example, will be selected when most members are close to the group's average on the dependent variable. The AID analysis tells which groups are numerically or volumetrically most important for an overall market. It does this by displaying group size and average purchase volume for each significant grouping.

The AID technique assumes that the fit obtained is reliable. That is, the same results would be obtained if the analysis were performed again on an independent sample. The output from an AID program shows a tree describing the groups that vary on the dependent measure. This tree is a branching diagram that presents results for groups defined by one variable, then by two variables, and so on. This tree shows the number of people in each group and the group's average performance on the dependent variable. The incidence of each group in the study sample also is provided.

Analysis 3.1. "Instant Curls" Electric Hairstyler

In Case 3.1, Instant Curls, one of the objectives of the study was to identify the target market for this product. The AID analysis was used to locate segments that account for a disproportionately high number of Instant Curls buyers. A key segment identified was women under 50; this group was large enough to warrant marketing support, and the incidence of purchase was highest in this group. The identification of women under 50 as the key segment was not surprising. But the estimated value of this group was critical for the planning of marketing effort levels against this group.

Discriminant Analysis

Discriminant analysis enables the researcher to predict group membership of individuals based on members' characteristics. For example, buyers of a certain make of car versus nonbuyers might be predicted on the basis of several life-style variables by means of this technique. The output of a discriminant analysis includes a display of the goodness of fit of the results—that is, the percentage of correct predictions for each group. This gives a good idea of how reliable the information may be to act on. The discriminant analysis output also presents a summary table that shows, in order of predictive power, the variables most important to the classification.

Discriminant function is a stepwise procedure that enters, successively, variables with the highest multiple correlation with the groups. The program enters one independent variable at a time. The result is the best collection of variables, in order of strength (or importance) that correlates with group membership.

Analysis 3.2. "Charge-Up" Nutrition Bar

In Case 3.2, Charge-Up, a discriminant analysis was used to predict attitudes of purchase resistance. Predisposition to buy Charge-Up was the dependent variable. Many variables were screened as predictors of buying predisposition. This analysis resulted in a reasonably successful application of this technique. Predictors of purchase resistance were statistically significant, and several actionable variables were identified, leading to specific marketing strategies.

COMPUTER ANALYSIS

A numerical example of the AID technique is provided in this section. The purpose of the analysis is to ascertain how the predictors explain variation in the dependent variable by means of a binary segmentation procedure.

Analysis Plan: AID

Each respondent is measured once on all the variables. There are four variables: Y, A, B, C. Y is the dependent variable, interval scaled from 1 to 9. The remaining (independent) variables are nominal, with levels as follows: $A = 2$, $B = 4$, $C = 3$. Referring to Table 3.1, line 1 shows each variable; line 2 indicates the name of these variables, and line 3 separates the independent variables from the dependent variables. The number of respondents is $n = 20$. See Table 3.1.

Computer Output

Table 3.2, Group Summary Table, shows the total number of groups generated by the AID analysis. It also indicates which of these groups are end points, that is, sufficiently homogeneous to avoid further splitting.

Line 1 names the group and gives its size (number of respondents). Line 2 shows the mean value of the dependent variable, Y, and its variance. Also, shown is SS(L)/TSS, an index of group homogeneity; and BSS/TSS, an index showing the proportion of group variation in Y that can be explained by a binary split. Line 3 shows the variable used to make the best split and BSS(L), the sums of squares involved in the split. Below this are shown the groups formed by the split and the classes of the split variable assigned to those groups. Line 5 shows one result of a split.

Interpretation

An AID tree based on the numerical example is shown in Figure 3.1. This tree shows the flow of the binary segmentation operation up to the third level of split. Each cell represents a group from the computer output of Table 3.2. The

TABLE 3.1   AID 3: Osiris Searching for Structure

AID3 : OSIRIS SEARCHING FOR STRUCTURE

AUTOMATIC INTERACTION DETECTOR – (OSIRIS BATCH)

1   THE VARIABLE LIST IS :

V1,V2,V3,V4

2   VAR.   TYPE   VARIABLE NAME

1   1   0   Y

1   2   0   A

1   3   0   B

1   4   0   C

3   YVAR=V1※

PRED=(V2,V3,V4) F END※

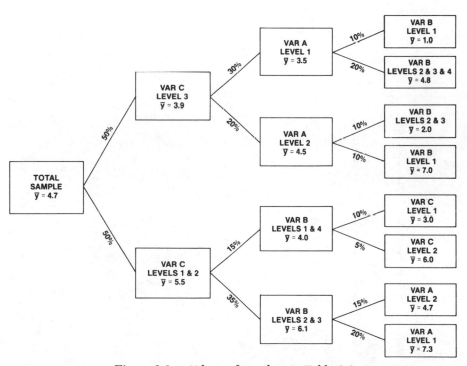

Figure 3.1.   Aid tree from data in Table 3.2.

41

TABLE 3.2 Group Summary Table (2 Sheets)

```
GROUP SUMMARY TABLE
23 GROUPS OF WHICH 12 ARE FINAL

GROUP   1 , N =    20, SUM W =  2.0000000E 01
Y MEAN= 4.700000E 00, VARIANCE= 8.642115E 00,   SS(L)/TSS= 1.000,  BSS/TSS= 0.078
SPLIT ON C          ,  BSS(L) = 1.2800005E 01   INTO
       2 WITH CLASSES 3
       3 WITH CLASSES 2  1

GROUP   2 , N =    10, SUM W =  1.0000000E 01
Y MEAN= 3.900000E 00, VARIANCE= 9.877780E 00,   SS(L)/TSS= 0.541,  BSS/TSS= 0.015
SPLIT ON A          ,  BSS(L) = 2.400024E 00    INTO
       4 WITH CLASSES 1
       5 WITH CLASSES 2

GROUP   3 , N =    10, SUM W =  1.0000000E 01
Y MEAN= 5.500000E 00, VARIANCE= 6.944444E 00,   SS(L)/TSS= 0.381,  BSS/TSS= 0.059
SPLIT ON B          ,  BSS(L) = 9.642822E 00    INTO
       6 WITH CLASSES 1  4
       7 WITH CLASSES 3  2

GROUP   4 , W =     6, SUM W =  6.0000000E 00
Y MEAN= 3.500000E 00, VARIANCE= 1.030000E 01,   SS(L)/TSS= 0.314,  BSS/TSS= 0.114
SPLIT ON B          ,  BSS(L) = 1.8750000E 01   INTO
       8 WITH CLASSES 1
       9 WITH CLASSES 4  2  3
```

```
GROUP   7 ,  N =     7, SUM W =  7.0000000E 00
Y MEAN= 6.142857E 00, VARIANCE= 7.476196E 00,    SS(L)/TSS=  0.273,  BSS/TSS=  0.070
SPLIT ON A                              , BSS(L) =  1.144043E 01   INTO
        10 WITH CLASSES   2
        11 WITH CLASSES   1

GROUP   5 ,  N =     4, SUM W =  4.0000000E 00
Y MEAN= 4.500000E 00. VARIANCE= 1.166667E 01,    SS(L)/TSS=  0.213,  BSS/TSS=  0.152
SPLIT ON B                              , BSS(L) =  2.500000E 01   INTO
        12 WITH CLASSES   2   3
        13 WITH CLASSES   1

GROUP   9*,  N =     4, SUM W =  4.0000000E 00
Y MEAN= 4.750000E 00, VARIANCE= 1.091667E 01,    SS(L)/TSS=  0.199,  BSS/TSS=  0.0

GROUP  11 ,  N =     4, SUM W =  4.0000000E 00
Y MEAN= 7.250000E 00, VARIANCE= 8.250000E 00,    SS(L)/TSS=  0.151,  BSS/TSS=  0.038
SPLIT ON B                              , BSS(L) =  6.250000E 00   INTO
        14 WITH CLASSES   3
        15 WITH CLASSES   2

GROUP  14*,  N =     2, SUM W =  2.0000000E 00
Y MEAN= 6.000000E 00, VARIANCE= 1.800000E 01,    SS(L)/TSS=  0.110,  BSS/TSS=  0.0

GROUP  10 ,  N =     3, SUM W =  3.0000000E 00
Y MEAN= 4.666666E 00, VARIANCE= 4.333344E 00,    SS(L)/TSS=  0.053,  BSS/TSS=  0.050
SPLIT ON C                              , BSS(L) =  8.166687E 00   INTO
        16 WITH CLASSES   2
        17 WITH CLASSES   1
```

Table 3.2 (continued)

GROUP 6 , N =   3, SUM W = 3.0000000E 00
Y MEAN= 4.000000E 00, VARIANCE= 4.000000E 00,   SS(L)/TSS= 0.049, BSS/TSS= 0.037
SPLIT ON C   , BSS(L) = 6.0000000E 00   INTO
        18 WITH CLASSES   1
        19 WITH CLASSES   2

GROUP 13*, N =   2, SUM W = 2.0000000E 00
Y MEAN= 7.000000E 00, VARIANCE= 8.000000E 00,   SS(L)/TSS= 0.049, BSS/TSS= 0.0

GROUP 18 , N =   2, SUM W = 2.0000000E 00
Y MEAN= 3.000000E 00, VARIANCE= 2.000000E 00,   SS(L)/TSS= 0.012, BSS/TSS= 0.012
SPLIT ON A   , BSS(L) = 2.0000000E 00   INTO
        20 WITH CLASSES   1
        21 WITH CLASSES   2

GROUP 12 , N =   2, SUM W = 2.0000000E 00
Y MEAN= 2.000000E 00, VARIANCE= 2.000000E 00,   SS(L)/TSS= 0.012, BSS/TSS= 0.012
SPLIT ON B   , BSS(L) = 2.0000000E 00   INTO
        22 WITH CLASSES   2
        23 WITH CLASSES   3

GROUP 16*, N =   2, SUM W = 2.0000000E 00
Y MEAN= 3.500000E 00, VARIANCE= 5.000000E-01,   SS(L)/TSS= 0.003, BSS/TSS= 0.0

GROUP 15*, N =   2, SUM W = 2.0000000E 00
Y MEAN= 8.500000E 00, VARIANCE= 5.000000E-01,   SS(L)/TSS= 0.003, BSS/TSS= 0.0

GROUP 8*, N =   2, SUM W = 2.0000000E 00
Y MEAN= 1.000000E 00, VARIANCE= 0.0   ,   SS(L)/TSS= 0.0 , BSS/TSS= 0.0

44

```
GROUP 20*, N =     1, SUM W =  1.0000000E 00
      Y MEAN= 2.0000000E 00, VARIANCE= 0.0        ,       SS(L)/TSS= 0.0    ,  BSS/TSS= 0.0

GROUP 22*, N =     1, SUM W =  1.0000000E 00
      Y MEAN= 1.0000000E 00, VARIANCE= 0.0        ,       SS(L)/TSS= 0.0    ,  BSS/TSS= 0.0

GROUP 23*, N =     1, SUM W =  1.0000000E 00
      Y MEAN= 3.0000000E 00, VARIANCE= 0.0        ,       SS(L)/TSS= 0.0    ,  BSS/TSS= 0.0

GROUP 19*, N =     1, SUM W =  1.0000000E 00
      Y MEAN= 6.000000 00, VARIANCE= 0.0          ,       SS(L)/TSS= 0.0    ,  BSS/TSS= 0.0

GROUP 21*, N =     1, SUM W =  1.0000000E 00
      Y MEAN= 4.0000000E 00, VARIANCE= 0.0        ,       SS(L)/TSS= 0.0    ,  BSS/TSS= 0.0

GROUP 17*, N =     1, SUM W =  1.0000000E 00
      Y MEAN= 7.0000000E 00, VARIANCE= 0.0        ,       SS(L)/TSS= 0.0    ,  BSS/TSS= 0.0
```

analysis shows how the overall sample is subdivided into subsamples that vary as much as possible in their average value on the dependent variable, Y. Figure 3.1 shows a range for Y of 3.9−5.5 for the first split. As the analysis progresses, Y is shown ranging from 1.0 to 7.3. Connecting lines show how the relative sizes of groups are formed. Note how at each level of branching, the proportions of the sample in the groups add to unity.

FOUR
Brand Loyalty Strategy

Brand loyalty is the likelihood that consumers will continue to purchase a brand they have tried. Brand loyalty information is needed for management decisions. These decisions include (1) whether to redevelop products or packages and (2) how much to spend to promote or reinforce favorable attitudes among present customers.

In Chapter 3 I covered the research necessary to explore consumer profiles, attitudes, and behavior for a brand's entire target market. Now, I show how brand loyalty studies sharpen the focus. This is done by studying a special group in the target market—consumers who purchase and use the brand.

The research you do improves a company's brand loyalty strategy. Here's how.

Provide support for product and packaging strategies. Through research, management checks its past decisions about products and packaging. If these decisions were right, the research on the brand will show it has high consumer satisfaction and repurchase. But sometimes the research will show that consumers do not like the product and purchase another brand. This may lead management to program changes in the product or package to improve brand loyalty.

Brand loyalty information, then, provides guidelines for the following:

Product Strategy. Reformulate along specific lines; when indicated, introduce line extensions or new products.

Packaging Strategy. Update packaging image and improve packaging communications.

You do different types of brand loyalty studies in support of product and packaging strategies. Exhibit 4.1 distinguishes some strategy research problems for brand loyalty that you must solve. Each of the problems concerns brand triers and is classified by whether the primary measurement is consumer attitude or consumer activity. Let's turn to the first of these research problems.

EXHIBIT 4.1   Examples of Brand Loyalty Strategy Problems

Research Problem	Study Sample	Primary Measurement
Meeting consumer needs	Brand triers	Consumer attitudes
Holding on to customers	Brand triers	Consumer activities

MEETING CONSUMER NEEDS

Knowing a consumer reaction to a brand after its use is essential to brand strategy. You fill this information gap by doing product acceptance studies. Product acceptance studies tell if consumers are satisfied with a brand after using it. Product acceptance will mean prepurchase doubts (such as questioning brand choice) will subside after the product's use. The aim is to market a product that performs at least as well as consumers had expected.

Product acceptance research provides important feedback on consumers' experiences with a product. The research you do determines that consumers' needs have been satisfied adequately or marginally or remain unsatisfied. If first-time and repeat triers are totally unsatisfied with the product's performance, the brand will not sustain itself in the marketplace for a prolonged period. In this case, management may decide it is not worthwhile investing in this brand.

Case Preview: "Pub's" Bloody Mary Mix

Case 4.1, Pub's, is an example where product management wondered whether the marketing effort to be invested in a brand was a worthwhile expenditure. This brand had been in the marketplace for six months and had received heavy advertising support. A similar product introduced by this manufacturer, Pub's Screwdriver Mix, had been very successful over the past year.

To evaluate the financial investment, the client asked its research company to measure Pub's Bloody Mary Mix acceptance among current users. The basic question asked was this: "Is 'Pub's Bloody Mary Mix' performance good enough to warrant marketing support?" This particular research company was selected for the project because it successfully handled the previous study for Pub's Screwdriver Mix. Therefore, it was in a position to perform the research so that the methods of the two studies were comparable.

A factor analysis used in this study showed that consumers evaluated Pub's Bloody Mary Mix according to three major criteria: taste, convenience, and appearance. The research showed that the product performed satisfactorily on these three factors, especially relative to Pub's Screwdriver Mix. Since the screwdriver mix was successful, Pub's Bloody Mary Mix was expected to have good repeat purchase and a favorable reputation among its triers. After the study was completed, the manufacturer concluded that the product was acceptable to consumers and warranted the contemplated investment.

Case 4.1   Reaction to "Pub's" Bloody Mary Mix Product

Objective

A new brand of Bloody Mary mix was introduced nationally six months ago. The objective of this study was to determine user reaction to the product.

Method

Telephone interviews, via Wide Area Telephone Service lines, were completed with 1420 brand users. Respondents were questioned about overall satisfaction, likes and dislikes, and usage habits. Additionally, the results of this study have been compared to the results of an earlier, similar study for a screwdriver mix whenever possible. A factor analysis of importance ratings was used to develop dimensions or criteria for evaluating the relative performances of Pub's Bloody Mary Mix and the Screwdriver Mix.

Recommendations and Conclusions

Three key factors were identified in the analysis as important for the evaluation of premixes for alcoholic beverages. These factors have been designated as taste, convenience, and appearance. Attributes associated with these factors are shown next, in order of their degree of association:

Taste	Convenience	Appearance
Alcohol blended evenly with mix	Simple to store ingredients	Looks inviting
Strength of mix	Takes a short time to prepare	Rich looking
Tastes like the real thing	Ingredients not quickly perishable	Has the right consistency
Spiciness	Easier to make than from scratch	Has a rich color

The average importance ratings of items in each factor suggest that taste (2.6) is most important, followed by appearance (2.3), then by convenience (2.2).

Having identified the key dimensions of evaluation, attribute ratings for Pub's Bloody Mary Mix and Pub's Screwdriver Mix were scaled into ratings of

the two products on taste, convenience, and appearance. This was accomplished by using factor scores.

   The Bloody Mary mix was found to be acceptable when the highly successful
Screwdriver mix is used as a standard of comparison. The Bloody Mary mix
scores much better on appearance, somewhat better on taste, and is about
equal on convenience. See Tables 1 and 2.

**TABLE 1   Factor Loadings for 13 Features of Alcoholic Beverage Premixes
(Based on Stated Importance Ratings)[a]**

Characteristics	Factor Loadings for Dimensions			Mean Importance Rating
	1 Taste	2 Convenience	3 Appearance	
1. Simple to store ingredients	.047	.642	−.089	1.83
2. Rich looking	.008	−.005	.584	2.62
3. Looks inviting	−.007	−.001	.764	2.42
4. Tastes like the real thing	.663	−.005	.020	3.27
5. Alcohol blended evenly with mix	.786	−.027	−.074	2.88
6. Looks like the real thing	−.003	−.009	.482	2.64
7. Has the right consistency	.004	− 050	.546	1.40
8. Ingredients not quickly perishable	.073	.526	−.009	1.68
9. Has a nice color	.014	.204	.441	2.53
10. Spiciness	.564	.056	.165	1.54
11. Takes a short time to prepare	−.069	.581	.116	2.81
12. Strength of the drink	.738	.046	.071	2.89
13. Easier to make than the real drink	.122	.427	.045	2.66

[a]Scale: 1 = extremely important; 2 = very important; 3 = fairly important; 4 = of little
importance.

TABLE 2   Ratings of Bloody Mary Mix and Screwdriver Mix (Based on Factor Scores for Three Dimensions of Importance)

	Factors		
	1	2	3
"Pub" Product	Taste	Convenience	Appearance
Bloody Mary Mix	.58	.42	.66
Screwdriver Mix	.43	.44	.32

The conclusion is that on an overall basis the Bloody Mary mix is a more-acceptable product than the Screwdriver mix. Additional information shows this:

On the Favorable Side

Levels of satisfaction for the product, in general, and for specific attributes were higher for the Bloody Mary mix than for the Screwdriver mix.

On the Negative Side

Over half the Bloody Mary mix users reported disliking something about the mix (but not quite as high as the responses for the Screwdriver mix). The most frequently mentioned dislike was taste—listed first by users of both mixes.

Nearly one-third of all Bloody Mary mix users indicated that they would definitely or probably would not repurchase (equal to the level for the Screwdriver mix users). Key reasons for not purchasing were price and poor mixability. See Table 3.

TABLE 3   Repurchase Intent

	Percentage	
Repurchase Intention	Bloody Mary Mix	Screwdriver Mix
Definitely would buy	31 ⎫	25 ⎫
Probably would buy	25 ⎬ 56	20 ⎬ 45
Might or might not buy	13	16
Probably would not buy	8	12
Definitely would not buy	24	16
Total	100	100
Base	(1420)	(1420)

Question: Which of the following statements best describes how you feel about buying this brand of Bloody Mary mix? Would you say . . . ?

TABLE 4   Reasons for Not Finishing the First Package of Bloody Mary or Screwdriver Mix

Those Who Did Not Finish Their First Packages	Percentage	
	Bloody Mary Mix	Screwdriver Mix
Negative reasons (net)	49	47
Unpleasant taste	38	16
Poor mixability	9	4
Did not agree with me or made me ill	26	19
Effectiveness (net)	5	11
Was not spicy enough	5	11
Neutral reason (net)	34	44
Stopped drinking Bloody Mary or Screwdriver Mix	17	25
Stopped drinking	—	6
Started diet	23	13
Medical reasons	5	—
Don't know	3	1
Total	100	100
Base	(550)	(680)

Question: Why would you say you have not finished your box of this mix?

Over one-third of those not finishing the first bottle of the Bloody Mary mix product cited taste as the reason. See Table 4.
Fully one-third of all Bloody Mary mix users indicated dissatisfaction with the product (equal to the Screwdriver mix level). See Table 5.

Among those who had previously used another mix, two-thirds of the mix users rated this mix better (compared to less than one-third for the Screwdriver mix users). See Table 6.

HOLDING ON TO CUSTOMERS

Some studies you do will measure whether consumers are so happy with a brand they've used that it will be repurchased. These are customer retention studies.

Customer retention studies, in addition to measuring repeat buying, may

TABLE 5 Satisfaction with "Pub's" Premixes

Overall Satisfaction	Percentage	
	Bloody Mary Mix	Screwdriver Mix
Satisfied	42	30
Not satisfied or dissatisfied	25	32
Dissatisfied	33	36
Don't know	—	2
Total	100	100
Base	(1420)	(1520)

Question: Overall, how satisfied are or were you with this brand of Bloody Mary or Screwdriver mix? Would you say . . . ?

TABLE 6 Evaluation of "Pub's" Premixes Relative to Others

Comparison to Other Brands	Percentage	
	Bloody Mary Mix	Screwdriver Mix
A lot better	48 ⎫	19 ⎫
	⎬ 66	⎬ 28
A little better	18 ⎭	9 ⎭
About the same	9	32
Not as good	25	30
Do not know	—	12
Total	69 = 100	73 = 100
Base	(640)	(730)

Question: On an overall basis, which statement best describes how this product compares with others you have tried? Would you say it is . . . ?

probe consumers' attitudes and perceptions that shape commitment to a brand. Because they uncover the basis of customer retention, the results of the studies you do aid in the development of advertising claims and possible shifts in product formulation. The studies are used as yardsticks for measuring the effectiveness of current marketing strategy.

Case Preview: "Studio 10" Tennis-Disco Club

Case 4.2, Membership Renewal in Studio 10 Tennis-Disco Club, was requested for aiding in development of strategies to increase club member retention rates. Earlier club research in a representative test area revealed problems in retaining present club members. The present research was conducted on a national scale among club members to uncover club members' attitudes, perceptions, and usage patterns. These findings measured retention for national club members and estimated retention rates under various ways the club could be marketed.

A predictive measure "conjoint analysis" showed that tennis court hours were by far the most important variable in renewals. This information provided specific marketing direction for improving renewal rates. A decision was made to lengthen the number of court hours available to members. Afterward, club membership retention rates increased markedly.

Case 4.2   Renewal in "Studio 10" Tennis-Disco Club

Objective

Studio 10's chain of tennis-disco clubs was introduced nationally. Prior to the national introduction, a follow-up study among members of the test market clubs was conducted in which the renewal level was found to be an unspectacular 55%. Research has therefore been conducted among national club members to determine the national renewal level and what can be done to improve that level.

Method

Telephone interviews were conducted nationally with 1500 club members. Conjoint analysis was used to measure the probable impact of membership options and privileges on measurement renewal.

Recommendations and Conclusions

A conjoint analysis explored these marketing alternatives to strengthen club membership: tennis court hours, number of disco nights, and membership costs. The analysis shows that membership renewals will be strengthened in a manner consistent with profit objectives by (1) setting membership costs at $40 per month, (2) offering members four hours a week in tennis court availability, and (3) four disco nights a month.

Tennis court hours are by far the most important variable in renewals, and the cost of making additional hours available is small relative to the overall budget for the franchise. The cost of additional disco nights is much greater, and the savings in having four rather than five disco nights is estimated to be greater than the anticipated revenues from increased renewals with five disco nights (see Tables 1 and 2 of this section).

Renewal Intention

Two-thirds of the respondents (67%) stated that they "definitely or probably" would renew their membership, as compared to 59% previously found in the test market. See Table 3.

Reasons for Joining the Club

The two major reasons were "run down or need exercise" and "want to meet new people." In comparison to the test market, the latter reason was cited more often and "run down or need exercise" was cited less often. See Table 4.

Overall Satisfaction Rating

About three-fifths (59%) of the respondents stated that they were "extremely" or "very" satisfied with the club. This is above the level of 44% in the test market. See Table 5.

TABLE 1   Values of Factors Affecting Membership Renewal in "Studio 10"
(Attribute Component Functions from Conjoint Analysis)

Attribute	Level	Value of Function
1. Tennis court hours	2/week	−1.034
	3/week	.983
	4/week	1.826
2. Disco nights	3/month	−.064
	4/month	.231
	5/month	.440
3. Membership costs	$40/month	.813
	$60/month	.128
	$80/month	−.907
Stress = 0.008		

TABLE 2   Plot of Factors Affecting Membership Renewal in Studio 10, Based on Additive Conjoint Measurement.

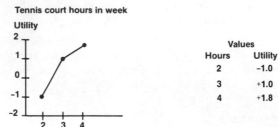

Values	
Hours	Utility
2	–1.0
3	+1.0
4	+1.8

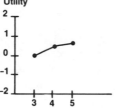

Values	
Nites	Utility
3	+0.0
4	+1.5
5	+1.7

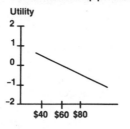

Values	
Monthly Cost	Utility
$40	+1.8
$60	± 0.0
$80	–1.6

Likes and Dislikes

About four-fifths (78%) of the respondents liked something about the club. As was found in the test market, the most frequently mentioned likes related to "feel good, better, less tired," "easy to meet people," and "good facilities." See Table 6.

One quarter of the respondents (24%) disliked something about the club, the main complaint being "too expensive." This was also the case for the test market data. See Table 7.

TABLE 3 Renewal Intention for Tennis-Disco Club

	Percentage	
Renewal Intention	National Club Members	Test Market Club Members
Definitely would	30 ⎫	29 ⎫
Probably would	37 ⎭ 67	30 ⎭ 59
Might or might not	18	12
Probably would not	7	24
Definitely would not	9	5
Base	(1500)	(1500)

Question: Which of the following statements best describes how you feel about rejoining the club in the next year? Would you . . . ? (Check list.)

TABLE 4 Reasons for Joining the Tennis-Disco Club

	Percentage	
Reasons for Joining Club	National Club Members	Test Market Club Members
Run-down feeling or need exercise	39	45
Want to meet new people	36	29
Like combination of tennis-disco club or innovative ideas	16	12
Friend recommended	5	9
Advertising	4	5
Base	(1500)	(1500)

Question: Why did you initially join this tennis-disco club?

TABLE 5 Overall Satisfaction with the Tennis-Disco Club

	Percentage	
Overall Satisfaction	National Club Members	Test Market Club Members
Extremely satisfied	22 ⎫	16 ⎫
Very satisfied	37 ⎬ 59	28 ⎬ 44
Somewhat satisfied	16	14
Somewhat dissatisfied	22	24
Very dissatisfied	11	10
Extremely dissatisfied	2	8
Base	(1500)	(1500)

Question: Overall, how satisfied are you with this tennis-disco club? Would you say you are . . . ? (Check list.)

TABLE 6 Likes of the Tennis-Disco Club

	Percentage	
Responses	National Club Members	Test Market Club Members
Respondents who liked something	78	85
Feel good, less tired, more energy	39	34
Easy to meet new people	16	26
Like combination of tennis-disco club	15	18
Like facilities	8	7
Respondents who liked nothing	22	15
Base	(1500)	(1500)

Question: What, if anything, do you like most about the tennis-disco club?

TABLE 7   Dislikes of the Tennis-Disco Club

	Percentage	
Responses	National Club Members	Test Market Club Members
Respondents who disliked something	24	18
Too expensive	15	10
Doesn't give energy or uplift	5	4
Difficult to meet people	2	3
Dislike facilities	2	1
Respondents who disliked nothing	76	82
Base	(1500)	(1500)

Question: What, if anything, do you dislike most about the tennis-disco club?

Age Profile

The age profile of the members appears to be older on a national basis than was found in the test market. See Table 8.

TABLE 8   Age Profile

	Percentage	
Age of Respondents	National Club Members	Test Market Club Members
Under 25	17 ⎫	30 ⎫
25–34	35 ⎭ 52	31 ⎭ 61
35–44	26	24
45–54	17	10
55 and over	4	5
Refused to give age	1	—
Base	(1500)	(1500)

SUMMARY

Brand loyalty strategy research measures the likelihood of repurchase among brand triers. These studies are used by decision makers in product and packaging areas. The decisions include (1) product reformulation, (2) new market entry, and (3) improvement of package communications and image.

Brand loyalty strategy research describes satisfaction and repurchase among brand triers in the marketplace. It evaluates after-use experiences and profiles a product's strengths and weaknesses. A basic question asked of you is this: "What can we learn that could improve my brand's loyalty rate?" Consumers are likely to continue purchasing the brand if they are satisfied after a trial use. If triers are unsatisfied, the brand will vanish from the marketplace.

All marketing strategy studies are broad in scope; each one covers several areas of the marketing mix. The results of marketing strategy studies are used to locate a variety of problems in a brand's marketing mix. The next chapters examine the kinds of research that probe only one special problem at a time.

TECHNICAL APPENDIX

ALTERNATE DESIGNS FOR BRAND LOYALTY STRATEGY RESEARCH

Design Alternatives	Notes
Unit of analysis Category user Category purchaser Company brand user Company brand purchaser	Brand loyalty studies sample company brand users. Often users of competitive brands are studied as a yardstick.
Data collection method Personal Telephone Mail	It is difficult to cluster users. Personal interviews used; but for large-scale studies, telephone and mail data collection become much more cost efficient for the sample obtained.
Stimulus presentation Brand unidentified Brand identified	Brand-identified stimuli are introduced when there is a need to avoid respondent confusion over a brand's types and forms.

Design Alternatives	Notes

Consumer response
   Monadic
   Repeat
	Single measures used to develop information about satisfaction and repurchase. Repeat measures may be used to obtain data on long-term brand loyalty and depth of repurchase.

Evaluation criteria
   Competitor brands
   Company brand
	Typically, evaluation involves competitors as a frame of reference.

ANALYTICAL TECHNIQUES

This section covers techniques used in the brand loyalty strategy research cases of this chapter. The presentation includes factor analysis and conjoint analysis. These techniques are multivariate; they typically involve three or more variables as a system. Factor and conjoint analyses are also interdependence methods, that is, grouping techniques.

Interdependence multivariate techniques provide marketing direction when (1) there are many marketing alternatives to consider and (2) greater marketing insight is needed into the basic pattern of consumer attitudes and activities.

Factor Analysis

Factor analysis is a method of creating a relatively small set of variables from a larger set.* This is accomplished by using a linear combination of the original measures. This linear combination shows how each variable relates to each factor. Factors derived from this analysis are relatively independent of each other. A factor analysis procedure rotates the factors in space so that the researcher can interpret the information. The rotation more clearly identifies each variable with its own factor.

A factor can be viewed as a cluster of variables. In market research practice, this cluster of variables is often used to provide an overall description of a brand's image and its product attribute performance. Looking at a few factors makes the information much easier to interpret in contrast to looking at a far larger number of individual variables.

*There are two types of basic factor analysis: *R* factor analysis (grouping variables) and *Q* factor analysis (grouping people). This discussion of factor analysis covers the *R* factor analysis procedure used in Case 4.1.

Analysis 4.1. "Pub's" Bloody Mary Mix

In Case 4.1, Pub's Bloody Mary Mix, three factors were identified from 13 variables measuring the importance of product features. The three factors explained most of the variance, and, therefore, the analysis stopped at that point. These three factors were most important to the understanding of product acceptance.

Conjoint Analysis

Conjoint analysis is a technique used to measure preferences as they are affected by a systematic presentation of attribute combination alternatives. For example, an airline can offer three price levels and three types of service (e.g., luxury and first and second class). Preferences for each of the nine combinations of prices and services would be ranked by respondents as input to the conjoint analysis. The output would be scaled values corresponding to the ranked data that were input. The scaled values are called utilities; the higher the value of these utilities, the more important is the specific price or service to consumers' preferences. A "stress" statistic in the output would tell how well the conjoint model worked.

Analysis 4.2. "Studio 10" Tennis-Disco Club

In Case 4.2, Studio 10, three attributes were singled out for a conjoint analysis to determine what could be done about improving membership renewal in a club. The analysis provided an excellent fit to the conjoint model, as shown by a low stress value (*stress* is a badness of fit of the conjoint model to the data). The study found that tennis court hours are the most important marketing variable. This led to an important marketing decision to change the terms of club membership to make renewal more attractive.

COMPUTER ANALYSIS

A numerical example of factor analysis by principal components is presented in this section. The purpose of the analysis is to partition the total variance in a set of variables into uncorrelated elements or principal components.

Analysis Plan: Principal Components Factor Analysis

There are three variables: *A*, *B* and *C*. These are treated as interdependent. Each respondent is measured three times, once on each variable. The scale in every case is $1-11$. Table 4.1 shows the 30 scores in the analysis. Also shown is

TABLE 4.1   Principal Components Factor Analysis

TITLE 'FACTOR ANALYSIS BY PRINCIPAL COMPONENTS';

DATA SASBATCH;

OBS	A	B	C
1	7	4	3
2	4	1	8
3	6	3	5
4	8	6	1
5	8	5	7
6	7	2	9
7	5	3	3
8	9	5	8
9	7	4	5
10	8	2	2

CORRELATION MATRIX

		A	B	C
1	A	1.00000	0.66866	−0.10131
2	B	0.66866	1.00000	−0.28793
3	C	−0.10131	−0.28793	1.00000

a correlation matrix: intercorrelations with A, B, and C are found on lines 1, 2, and 3, respectively.

Computer Output

Table 4.2 shows the results of the principal components factor analysis. On line 1, "eigenvalues" are shown for each of three principal factors. *Eigenvalues* are the roots of a characteristic equation. They are used as a measure of the variance that a given dimension contributes.

Lines 2 and 3 show the amounts of the total variance explained by each factor individually and on a cumulative basis. The ratio of the eigenvalues for each factor to the sum of the eigenvalues (the trace) provides the information for "portion."

Line 4, "Factor Pattern," indicates a matrix that shows correlations between factors and variables.

TABLE 4.2   Principal Components Factor Analysis

FACTOR ANALYSIS BY PRINCIPAL COMPONENTS

✕✕SAS SPEC

PRIOR ESTIMATES OF COMMUNALITY

	A	B	C
	1.000000	1.000000	1.000000

		1	2	3
1	EIGENVALUES	1.768774	0.927076	0.304150
2	PORTION	0.590	0.309	0.101
3	CUM PORTION	0.590	0.899	1.000

4   FACTOR PATTERN

	FACTOR1	FACTOR2	FACTOR3
A	0.85384	0.37038	-0.36576
B	0.91283	0.09352	0.39749
C	-0.45440	0.88383	0.11122

FINAL COMMUNALITY ESTIMATES:

	A	B	C
	1.000000	1.000000	1.000000

5   SCORING COEFFICIENT MATRIX

	FACTOR1	FACTOR2	FACTOR3
A	0.48273	0.39952	-1.20257
B	0.51608	0.10088	1.30689
C	-0.25690	0.95335	0.36567

Line 5, "Scoring Coefficient Matrix," heads an array that gives the loadings of each variable for each factor. These are used as weights for obtaining factor scores, if desired.

Interpretation

The analysis of Table 4.2 shows the principal components factor analysis for scaled variables A, B, and C. Eigenvalues obtained for the three factors are 1.768774, 0.927076, and 0.304150. The cumulative contributions to the total variance are 0.590 for factor 1, 0.899 for factors 1 and 2, and 1.000 for all three factors.

The correlations of variables with factors—the factor pattern—shows the following: variable A (0.85384) has a high positive correlation with factor 1 and a moderate negative correlation on factor 3 (-0.36576). Variable B (0.91283) is highly correlated with factor 1 and moderately (0.39749) with factor 3. Both correlations are positive. Variable C has a moderate negative correlation (0.45440) with factor 1 and a high correlation (0.88383) with factor 2. Weights for scoring individuals on each factor are described in the factor pattern table.

PART THREE

PRODUCT RESEARCH

FIVE
Product Concept Viability

The appeal of a product concept determines the maximum number of consumers who will try a brand. A product concept gives information for making choices about a specific product or service. An example of a product concept is "a children's vitamin that supplies minerals found in vegetables—for children who don't like vegetables." *Product concept viability* is the concept's power to persuade consumers that one particular product should be chosen over its alternatives.

Research done on product concept viability should dovetail with marketing strategy research. I stated in Chapters 3 and 4 that consumer needs and habits are described in marketing strategy studies. Research for product concept viability tests reactions to concepts designed to meet specific needs and to fit existing habit patterns.

This chapter shows how research can identify good product concepts. Those concepts meeting the test of the research you do may become sales messages in the marketplace. Let's see what you accomplish when you weigh the viability of a product concept.

Test product concepts quickly, economically, and without executional bias. Product concepts are seemingly endless. Research opens a company's options by permitting the evaluation of several alternatives at the idea stage. The results of product concept viability studies can be available a few weeks from the time a study is commissioned. As is well known, marketing that outpaces what competitors are doing creates a distinct advantage. And the cost of product concept viability research is relatively small when compared to the cost of testing a commercial or final print ad. In addition to being quick and economical, product concept viability research permits a test of the sales message alone. Executional elements present in advertising copy—music, voice-overs, crawl, and so on—do not confound results.

Rate product concept viability and analyze its appeal and market. This basic question is asked, "How good is the idea?" The research conducted tests various possibilities. Up-front research leads to go/no-go and hold-and-revise decisions for product and communications development. Beyond screening for

EXHIBIT 5.1.   Examples of Product Concept Viability Problems

Research Problems	Marketing Ideas
Replacing product concepts	Several concepts — current product
Selecting line extension concepts	Several concepts — related product
Finding concepts for new products	Several concepts — new products
Naming brands	Several names for one concept — new product

good ideas, research contributes much more. The data you gather are used to do the following:

Analyze the appeal for key benefits, reasons why.

Refine the target market definition and anticipate the competitive field of brands.

The rating you give a product concept, based on research, helps to identify promising marketing ideas. Other factors are brought into play before action is taken: sales force coverage, cost of goods, and the like.

You identify effective marketing ideas in a variety of product concept viability studies such as those shown in Exhibit 5.1. This exhibit, however, cites specific product concept viability research problems. The individual research problem is classified by answering two questions: (1) Are several concepts or several names for one concept being dealt with? (2) Is the product current, related, or new? Let's explore each of these research problems.

REPLACING PRODUCT CONCEPTS

A mature brand may acquire a stale, tired image among consumers. When this happens, it is time to think about replacing the brand's product concept. *Marketers will consider a variety of concepts that are possibly useful for revitalizing an ongoing brand. The job you have is to select the best of several concepts considered for this brand.*

Suppose you have determined that a brand's current image is questionable or unfavorable. Marketing's objective, then, is to select one new concept that can favorably change consumers' perceptions of a brand. In so doing, the brand attracts desired segments.

On the other hand, the marketing strategy research and other data sources can indicate that the brand's image is favorable and attracts desired market segments. In this case, marketing's objective is to select brand concepts that further strengthen and reinforce the brand's current image among consumers.

By testing new concepts you show how an on-market brand can (1) better focus its relevance to a new consumer segment, (2) reorder emphasis on its special benefits, (3) highlight new usage occasions for it, or (4) redefine its product field of competition.

Case Preview: "Commence" Car Batteries

Case 5.1, Commence, was requested as follow-up research after a brand strategy study. The latter study concluded that the brand's position was highly vulnerable, relative to two new competitive entries. An earlier tracking study had revealed that two years preceding the market entry of these two new competitive brands, Commence car battery was rated the leading brand in the field. Then the brand's leadership eroded. The researcher recommended to brand management that a study be launched to replace Commence's product concept. The aim of the proposed study was to help find a way to improve the brand's sales trend. The researcher suggested, as a first step, that new concepts for Commence be developed and evaluated.

The advertising agency responsible for creating these new concepts commissioned its research supplier to do qualitative research on the subject. Focus groups that were conducted among car owners or maintainers provided direction for the development of three new concepts. One concept emphasized a written guarantee; another emphasized endorsement by cops; the third concept emphasized that this car battery was reliable enough to be used in Grand Prix racing. This last concept represented the approach used in the brand's current advertising.

These three concepts were tested among car owners or maintainers. A completely randomized analysis of variance (ANOVA) was used to test for differences between the concepts' average purchase intent scores. The analysis showed that the "guarantee" battery concept was the strongest of the three concepts tested. The other two concepts were found by a Newman-Keuls test to be not significantly different from each other.

As a result of this research, it was decided to replace the brand's concept, using the "guarantee" theme. The research illustrated that the current concept was not as appealing as might have been assumed; earlier study and action might have enabled the brand to have retained its dominant market share. The case shows that concept research is one important means for quickly turning around an unfavorable sales trend.

Case 5.1   Test of Three Concepts for "Commence" Car Batteries

Objective

Three different car battery concepts were tested among adult male car owners or maintainers to measure differences, if any, in buying motivations that relate to these three concepts:

A battery that "had a written guarantee that you'd get three years' use" (guarantee).

A battery that "was recommended by State Highway Patrolmen as the best battery ever used in their patrol cars" (cops).

A battery that "was the only regular automobile battery reliable enough to compete in Grand Prix car racing" (able to race).

Method

A telephone survey among car owners or maintainers was conducted. The sample of the 600 respondents was divided into three equal groups of 200 each. Each respondent was limited to answering questions about one concept only, the concept exposed, on a randomly assigned basis.

Respondents were asked to rate the concept to which they were exposed. Ratings were given on a 10-point purchase intent scale. A completely randomized analysis of variance was used to test for differences between the concepts' average purchase intent scores. A Newman-Keuls test was used to make specific comparisons of means.

Recommendations and Conclusions

The "guarantee" car battery concept outscores the other two concepts and clearly establishes itself as the strongest of three concepts tested. Therefore, "guarantee" is recommended for use in a new advertising campaign that is to be tested in a limited area of the United States.

An analysis of variance and comparison test shows that there is a significant overall difference between average purchase interest for the battery concepts researched. The best-scoring concept is "three-year guarantee" (5.27). The weaker scoring concepts ("cop," 4.42; and "able to race," 4.28) are found by a Newman-Keuls test not to be significantly different from each other (see Tables 1–3).

Purchase intent for the "guarantee," "cop," and "able to race" concepts was analyzed on a closeness (in time) to purchase basis (the next time they expect to buy a car battery). The data show that those respondents who expect to buy

TABLE 1.   Average Purchase Intent for Three Concepts for "Commence" Car Batteries

	Average Purchase Intent	
Concept Tested	10-Point Scale	Base
Guarantee	5.27	(200)
Cop	4.42	(200)
Able to race	4.28	(200)

TABLE 2.   Sources of Variation in Purchase Intent for Three Concepts for "Commence"

Sources of Variation	MS (Mean Square)	F	df	Significance Level
Concepts	251.72	10.97	2	$P < .001$
Error	22.72		597	
Total			599	

TABLE 3.   Comparisons of Purchase Intent Averages for Three Concepts for "Commence" Car Batteries [a]

Concept		Guarantee	Cop	Able to Race
	Average Purchase Intent	5.27	4.42	4.28
Guarantee	5.27	—	.85	.99
Cop	4.42		—	.14
Able to race	4.28			—
		Guarantee	Cop	Able to Race

[a] Newman-Keuls critical values (CV): $CV_2 = .46$, $CV_3 = .37$. Any two averages not underscored by the same horizontal line are significantly different at $P < .05$.

earlier, especially within the next year, have a higher interest in the "guarantee" concept. Similarly, the farther off in time the next purchase is planned, the more the score for the "able to race" concept is seen to increase at the expense of the "guarantee" concept. The inference is that the closer to the expected time of purchase one is, the stronger the pull of the "guarantee" concept.

The same conclusion does not hold for the "cop" concept; the "guarantee" concept is consistently superior to "cop" concept. However, interest in the "cop" concept bears little relationship to expected time of purchase. Therefore, the "guarantee" concept has a stronger advantage when the subgroups who expect to buy sooner are compared. Thus the "guarantee" concept's superiority is supported by its apparently greater strength over the other concepts among purchasers who are more likely to enter the market in the near future. See Table 4.

The amount of money one expects to spend for the next car battery purchase ($60 or under or over $60/battery) does not seem to be related to concept preference. See Table 5.

TABLE 4.   Purchase Intent for "Commence" Car Battery Concepts by Closeness (in Time) to Point of Purchase

Concepts	Total	Buying Periods (in months)			
		6	6–12	12–15	15 or More
Guarantee	5.27	5.57	5.51	5.22	5.16
Cop	4.42	4.45	4.48	4.39	4.42
Able to race	4.28	4.04	4.12	4.31	4.64

Question: When do you expect to buy a car battery again:
   Within the next 6 months?
   Within 6 months to a year?
   Within the next 12 to 15 months?
   15 months or after?

TABLE 5.   Purchase Intent for "Commence" Car Battery Concepts (by Estimated Cost — $60 or Under or Over — of Next Car Battery Purchase)

Concepts	Total	$60 or Under	Over $60
Guarantee	5.27	5.25	5.29
Cop	4.42	4.43	4.40
Able to race	4.20	4.26	4.29

Question: How much do you expect to pay the next time you purchase a car battery?

SELECTING LINE EXTENSION CONCEPTS

Often product concepts for existing brands are quite viable. It is best, perhaps, to select concepts for new products—concepts bearing generic brand names with existing products. This unit covers line extensions: new variations of an established brand's product, for example, a new flavor of soda to complement flavors currently marketed for an existing brand.

Brand management's objective is to introduce a line extension that will (1) attract new customers to the brand and (2) increase brand share. To do so, "cannibalization," or the "transfer" of sales from a main brand to a line extension, must be minimized.

Keeping these marketing objectives in mind, the ideal research design will include measures of the line extension's performance:

The consumer's ability to differentiate the line extension from the main product.

The line extension's appeal.

The line extension's appeal among current brand users, former brand users, and potential brand users.

If the study you conduct reveals that the line extension has its greatest appeal among current brand users, research may recommend not marketing the line extension because of the problem of cannibalization discussed earlier. The main brand concept may be incompatible with a line extension concept. If the latter concept has merit, marketing may choose to test its viability as an entirely new brand.

Case Preview: Television Model Concept

Case 5.2, "CVC," is an example of a line extension concept that also represented an entry into a new category. Marketers at CVC wanted information and estimates about this line extension—a TV set with a radio add-on feature. They wanted to know (before committing expenses) if a sufficiently large base of consumers were interested in purchasing the TV. This study did not consider the main brand's image, nor did it segment the TV market by brand purchased; it focused on general consumer reaction to the concept for a TV set with a radio add-on feature.

Marketers at CVC believed that their main brand had a positive "modern technology, innovative" image among consumers. They felt that this image would support acceptance of the proposed line extension. They wanted a "short" study that limited itself to the measurement of purchase interest in the line extension concept among adult TV purchasers. The researcher suggested to the marketers that the study be broadened in scope to permit analysis of response by additional market segments, say, hi-fi radio purchasers. Also, the researcher suggested that the study assess the compatibility of the line extension and main brand. The suggestions were considered but rejected, and the study proceeded.

The research concluded that purchase interest for the concept relative to purchase interest for the main brand was not strong enough to warrant further development of the line extension. Based on the research, the marketing department tabled the project.

Case 5.2   Potential for a "CVC" Television Model Concept

Objective

Marketing is currently considering development, for possible market testing, of a television set with a radio add-on feature. If its appeal is strong enough, the product will be introduced during the Christmas gift season. This market entry has tentatively been given the brand name Radio-Vision.

The purpose of this study is to determine whether this innovation has sufficient marketing potential to warrant proceeding.

Method

The total sample size was 300 consumers, ages 18–65 who had purchased a TV in the past year. Respondents were selected randomly to form a single experimental group of Radio-Vision prospects. Exposure to the items involved observing, viewing, and hearing actual models that were tagged with descriptive literature. Exposure was on a "dyadic basis" so that each respondent was exposed to two product concepts. The order of exposure was assigned randomly.

As a minimum guideline for decision making, the Radio-Vision concept at its price had to significantly outscore a control concept for standard TV. The control concept was for a mass appeal item at the average market price for standard TVs. A randomized block within-subjects analysis of variance was used to test for differences in purchase interest. The final decision was to be made by marketing, taking into account additional factors, including manufacturing costs and lead times.

Recommendations and Conclusions

Radio-Vision, the TV with a radio add-on feature, as presently conceived is not recommended; it fails to meet the decision criterion.

Average purchase intent for Radio-Vision (2.23) is not significantly higher than the average for the standard set concept (2.54). An analysis of variance shows that observed differences between the concepts are not significant. See Tables 1 and 2.

Positive purchase intent levels of 7% are found for the TV with the radio add-on feature and 17% for the standard TV. Not a single respondent said she or he "would definitely buy" either item. A relatively high proportion of respondents fall into the neutral intent category: 41% for the TV with the radio add-on feature and 35% for the standard TV set. See Table 3.

Respondents tend to like the convenience of having a radio and TV together. Almost half of the women exposed to the TV with a radio add-on feature (45%) comment favorably about the convenience of having the two items (TV and

TABLE 1. Average Purchase Intent for Radio-Vision and Standard TV Concepts

Concept	Average Purchase Intent (5-Point Scale)	Base
Radio-Vision	2.23	
Standard set	2.54	(300)

TABLE 2. Sources of Variation in Purchase Intent for Radio-Vision versus Standard TV

Sources of Variation	MS = Mean Square	F	df	Significance Level
Concepts	20.64	2.94	1	N.S.($P > .05$) [not significant]
Respondents			299	
Concepts × Respondents	7.02		299	
Total			599	

TABLE 3. Purchase Intentions for a TV with a Radio Add-On Feature and a Standard TV

Purchase Intention	Percentage	
	Radio-Vision	Standard TV
Definitely would buy	—	—
Probably would buy	7	17
Might or might not buy	35	41
Probably would not buy	32	21
Definitely would not buy	26	21
Total	100	100
Base	(300)	(300)

Question: Here is a model of a product. Supposing it was available in your store; which of the following statements best describes how likely you would be to purchase this item?

radio) together. Related to this, 32% says you "can buy one unit instead of making two purchases," and 13% feels that "the size is good." See Table 4.

A high proportion of respondents exposed to the TV with the radio add-on feature feel that the screen is too small. About one-fourth of this sample (26%) feels that the screen is too small, and 19% perceives the radio speakers as too small. Nineteen percent does not like the item's concept, and 13% feels that the set is "poorly made or cheap looking." See Table 5.

Over half of the respondents exposed to the standard TV react favorably to the set's reception. When asked what, if anything, they liked about the set, over half of the exposed sample (52%) mention the reception. Other aspects receiving a favorable response are that you "can play it anywhere" (41%), "the fact that it has transistors," (38%) and the "convenience of usage in a den or TV room" (35%). See Table 6.

Respondents' dislikes about the standard TV are reported as follows: over one-fourth (28%) says that this TV is too big; 24% of the same sample says that the item is too small. About one-fourth of this sample feels that the remote tuner could break. Still other negative mentions relate to general rejection of the standard TV (17%) and the unacceptable reception (14%). See Table 7.

TABLE 4.   Aspects Liked about the TV with the Radio Add-On Feature

Aspect	Percentage Liking
Liked convenience of having radio and TV together	45
Buy one unit instead of two separate purchases	32
Good size	13
Other mentions	28[a]
Total[b]	
Base	(300)

Question: What, if anything, did you like about this item?

[a] No other single mention given by more than two respondents.
[b] Adds to more than 100% because of multiple mentions.

TABLE 5.   Aspects Disliked about the TV with the Radio Add-On Feature

Aspect	Percentage Disliking
Screen is too small	26
Radio speakers are too small	19
Don't like the concept	19
Poorly made or cheap looking	13
Too expensive	10
Unit is too big	10
Other mentions	35[a]
Total[b]	
Base	(300)

Question: What, if anything, did you dislike about this TV with the radio add-on feature?

[a] No other single mention given by more than two respondents.
[b] Adds to more than 100% because of multiple mentions.

TABLE 6.   Aspects Liked about the Standard TV

Aspects	Percentage Liking
Like the quality of the reception	52
Play it anywhere	41
It has transistors	38
Use in a den or TV room	35
Looks sturdy	27
Good looking	21
Good for the beach	21
Slots are attractive	14
Good size	14
Other mentions	21[a]
Liked nothing	21
Total[b]	
Base	(300)

Question: What, if anything, did you like about this item?

[a] No other single mention given by more than two respondents.
[b] Adds to more than 100% because of multiple mentions.

TABLE 7.   Aspects Disliked about the Standard TV

Aspects	Percentage Disliking
It is too big	28
It is too small	24
Remote tuner	24
Do not like the concept	17
Do not like the quality of reception	14
Ugly, homely, unattractive	10
It's too expensive	10
Does not seem sturdy	10
Other mentions	27[a]
Total[b]	
Base	(300)

[a] No other single mention given by more than two respondents.
[b] Adds to more than 100% because of multiple mentions.

In conclusion, most of the negative responses appear to be related to the specific product and not necessarily to the general concept itself. It is possible that a more aesthetically appealing set or variety of sets (possibly available at a higher price to strengthen the quality image) would result in a more-favorable purchase disposition.

FINDING CONCEPTS FOR NEW PRODUCTS

In time, marketing will have proliferated its line of products under existing brand names. Further growth then requires marketing new, unrelated products under new brand names.

New product concepts may be classified according to whether they (1) fit into an existing product category or (2) open up an entirely new category. *Concepts for existing product categories are expected to free users from concerns and dissatisfactions with existing products.* Selecting the target market is difficult when a concept is designed for a new category. *Concepts for new product categories are expected to meet unfulfilled consumer needs—those difficult to document.* These needs may not have been clearly identified in prior research.

Frequently, a product concept by itself (without a name) is used when the aim is to find concepts for a new product. In some cases, however, you, the researcher, are asked to evaluate a new brand name and concept as a totality.

Case Preview: "Stratford" Sewing Machine

In Case 5.3, Stratford, research was requested by a company interested in entering an existing product market: sewing machines. Secondary sources indicated that users of this product category were concentrated in the 18—54 age range; the latter was identified as the target market, and this description became the screen for the study. In addition, qualified respondents were screened for positive purchase interest in a sewing machine. Stratford had never marketed sewing machines but had manufactured different types of sewing needles and threads.

The specific objective of this study was to determine which of eight concepts was the most viable. Research assisted marketing and the advertising agency in creating these eight product concepts. The researcher did a content analysis of the competitive advertising. The analysis was used for creating some product concepts, eliminating others.

The split-plot analysis of variance showed that the sewing machine concepts differed significantly in the levels of purchase interest they generated. One of the eight concepts, *Designing a new you,* was the clear winner. It was recommended for marketplace use. This research shows how different concepts—for the same product—can significantly differ in the way they affect purchase interest from a statistical viewpoint.

Case 5.3   Evaluation of Concepts for a "Stratford" Sewing Machine

Objective

The Stratford Company is considering entry into the sewing machine market. The target age group has been specified as women 18—54.

Eight concepts for a new sewing machine product are in the developmental stage:

Be your own image maker.

Clothes restyler.

Sewing made simple.

A simple way to make a new wardrobe.

Restyling to suit him.

Designing your new wardrobe, inexpensively.

Designing a new you.

A simple-to-use sewing machine.

The objective of this final report is to recommend the most viable concept.

Method

Target-age respondents were screened for positive interest in purchasing a sewing machine. Each eligible respondent's self-rating on experience with sewing machines was obtained as well. A given respondent then was exposed to each of the eight test concepts and asked to rate purchase interest for each concept on a 100-point scale. Each concept was presented via an illustrated communications board. A split-plot, between-within ANOVA was computed to evaluate concept differences. Separate cells of 150 beginners and 150 persons experienced in using sewing machines were exposed to all eight test concepts on a random assignment basis. After concepts were shown to a given respondent, she was asked to evaluate the concepts by means of a purchase interest score.

To be considered for further development, a given concept's aggregate purchase score had to be at least at 50 on a 100-point purchase intent scale. If more than one concept met this criterion, research was to recommend the one concept that appeared to show the most potential.

Recommendations and Conclusions

The *Designing a new you* concept for Stratford sewing machines is the clear winner and is recommended for marketplace use. This concept registers an overall purchase score of 58%—the only sewing machine concept to score significantly higher than the recommended minimum score.

Moreover, *Designing a new you's* purchase score is the only one appreciably to surpass the criterion, among both beginners and those experienced at sewing.

A split-plot analysis of variance shows that the sewing machine concepts differ significantly in the levels of purchase interest. Sewing experience is found to be a significant variable, affecting interest in specific concepts. *Designing a new you* is stronger among women who are experienced at sewing than among beginners.

A Newman-Keuls test of differences between concepts in purchase interest confirms that *Designing a new you* is superior to the other seven concepts. See Tables 1–4.

Designing a new you has another important advantage. It is seen by 76% as being different from other products. In this respect, it is well above average for the eight concepts, but it is not significantly better than two of the other concepts: *Restyling to suit him* and *Own image maker*. See Table 5.

Respondents were asked to rate features of an ideal sewing machine and then to rate the Stratford machine on these same features. The Stratford machine appears to be a strong market entry, based on its generally close correspondence to the ideal, feature by feature. Although it has no serious deficiencies, Stratford has its biggest opportunity to improve its rating on the feature "does a variety of stitches," an area Stratford falls well below the ideal. "Ease of use" and "does a variety of stitches" are two of the most important attributes consumers want in a sewing machine. See Table 6.

NAMING BRANDS

A variety of brand names may seem suitable for a viable new product concept. A task for the marketer introducing a new product is to select an effective brand name. *Management wants a brand name that enhances product concepts, is memorable, and heightens the consumer's desire to purchase the product.* Names that are used in the research you use frequently are suggested by copy writers. These copy writers are thinking ahead to the name's usefulness in advertising strategy and execution.

Ideally, prospective brand names are expected to (1) create positive purchase interest, (2) improve response to a product concept by making the product characteristics that are appealing more salient, (3) suggest important competitive advantages, (4) be memorable, and (5) be relevant to the product concept. A name that does these things satisfactorily can be recommended for use in new product development.

Case Preview: "Simpson" Mattress Line

In Case 5.4, Simpson, the researcher was asked to design a study to test four names considered for a new mattress. The marketer had expressed interest in learning which of these four names emphasized the product's best quality: its superiority in giving a better quality of sleep.

The product was ready for the test market; only the name had to be settled on. Therefore, the researcher was being pressured to produce the results as soon as possible.

On the basis of the study's findings, SlumberJack was selected as the best

TABLE 1. Average Purchase Intent for Eight Concepts for a "Stratford" Sewing Machine (among Beginners at Sewing and Experienced at Sewing)

Experience Level	Average Purchase Intent (10-Point Scale)								
	Designing a New You	Restyling Your Clothes	Own Image Maker	Simple New Wardrobe	Simple to Use	Your New Wardrobe	Sewing Made Simple	Clothes Restyler	Base
Beginner at sewing	55.8	50.8	49.2	47.2	45.2	45.0	44.1	43.8	(150)
Experienced at sewing	60.4	53.6	52.6	51.2	48.8	42.4	36.5	33.1	(150)
Total	58.0	51.0	48.8	48.0	47.4	44.8	40.8	40.6	(300)

TABLE 2. Sources of Variation in Purchase Intent for Eight Concepts for a "Stratford" Sewing Machine

Sources of Variation	MS = Mean Square	F	df	Significance Level
Between				
respondents	—		299	
Sewing experience	35.07	5.47	1	$P < .05$
Error	6.41		298	
Within respondents			2100	
Concepts	172.59	17.72	7	$P < .01$
Sewing experience				
× concepts	13.25	1.36	7	N.S. $(P < .05)$
Error	9.74		2086	
Total			899	

name for this product. The study showed that different brand names can produce strong differences in potential trial, as indicated by purchase intent scores.

Case 5.4 Name Selection for a New "Simpson" Mattress Line

Objective

Simpson's marketing department is thinking of naming a new bed mattress line to emphasize its superiority in giving a better quality of sleep. As a means of reinforcing this concept, four names are proposed for the product. The purpose of this research is to recommend a name and its associated product concept for introducing the mattress product. The four product names or concepts tested are these:

SlumberJack.
SlumberJack by Simpson.
Sleepwell.
Sleepwell by Simpson.

Method

The objective was met by performing a survey among 200 people who were considering purchase of a new mattress over the next year. The overall sample was subdivided randomly into four separate groups of 50 each. Individual groups of respondents were exposed to two communication boards, one at a time—one of the four Simpson mattress names and a control name—a competitive brand. After being exposed to each stimulus, respondents were asked a series of questions.

TABLE 3. Comparisons of Differences in Purchase Intent for Eight Concepts for a "Stratford" Sewing Machine

Concept	Average Purchase Intent (100-point scale)	Designing a New You	Restyling Your Clothes	Own Image Maker	Simple New Wardrobe	Simple to Use	Your New Wardrobe	Sewing Made Simple	Clothes Restyler
Designing a new you	58.0	—	7.0	9.2	10.0	10.6	13.2	17.2	17.4
Restyling to suit him	51.0		—	2.2	3.0	3.6	6.2	10.2	10.4
Own image maker	48.8			—	0.8	1.4	4.0	8.0	8.2
Simple new wardrobe	48.0				—	0.6	3.2	7.2	7.4
Simple to sew	47.4					—	2.6	6.6	6.8
Your new wardrobe	44.8						—	4.0	4.2
Sewing made simple	40.8							—	0.2
Clother restyler	40.6								—

TABLE 4. Comparisons of Purchase Intent for Eight Concepts for a "Stratford" Sewing Machine

Designing a New You	Restyling Your Clothes	Own Image Maker	Simple New Wardrobe	Simple to Use	Your Own Wardrobe	Sewing Made Simple	Clothes Restyler
				___	___		
					___	___	

Newman-Keuls critical values $(CV)^a$:

$CV_2 = 3.8$ $CV_4 = 3.7$ $CV_6 = 4.1$
$CV_3 = 2.9$ $CV_5 = 5.4$ $CV_7 = 4.3$

[a] Any two averages not underscored by the same horizontal line are significantly different at $P < .05$.

86

TABLE 5.   Perception of "Stratford" Sewing Machine Concepts as Different from All Other Sewing Machine Products Ever Heard Of

Concept	Incidence of Respondents Perceiving Concept as Different from All Other Products (%)
Designing a new you	76
Restyling to suit him	74
Own image maker	73
Simple new wardrobe	56
Simple to use	56
Your new wardrobe	54
Sewing made simple	50
Clothes restyler	48
Base	(300)

TABLE 6.   Ratings of Features of the "Stratford" Sewing Machine as Compared with the Ideal Sewing Machine

Feature	Sewing Machine	
	Ideal	"Stratford"
Ease of use	8.36	8.22
Does a variety of stitches	8.01	5.36
Good for embroidery	7.22	6.81
Good for buttonholes	6.05	5.78
Good for different fabrics	5.81	5.69
Base	(300)	

For any one of the new names or concepts to be recommended, the name or concept had to score higher on the basis of purchase intent than the control name or concept. In deciding between the four test names, the key measure was a five-point purchase intent scale, using the ratio of

$$\frac{\text{Simpson name}}{\text{Control name}}$$

Analysis of score results showed that score data departed markedly from normal in their distributions. Therefore, the key measures were converted to rank data. Ranks were inverted so that a higher rank number represented a more favorable response. Significance tests were made by the Kruskal-Wallis technique.

Recommendations and Conclusions

The SlumberJack name, with its associated product concept, is recommended for introducing the new mattress product. Judging by the evaluative criterion (the ratio of positive purchase intent, test versus control) SlumberJack is superior to the remaining three name options.

The ranked scores show SlumberJack (183) well in front of the next leading name, SlumberJack by Simpson (102). A Kruskal-Wallis test finds this difference to be significant. Comparison of ranks by Ryan's procedure confirms that SlumberJack significantly outperforms each of the other test names on the basis of pairs. See Tables 1 and 2.

The major reasons for a positive purchase intent ("definitely" and "probably" will buy) for the test products concern the sleep benefit. A lack of differentiation between the test concept and existing products is important as a reason for negative purchase intent. See Table 3.

SUMMARY

Product concept viability research tells how enticing a brand is to consumers. This research can help decide which of several product ideas is most likely to succeed.

For existing brands, product concept viability research serves to (1) strengthen a favorable brand image, or (2) select a new concept for a new, better brand image.

TABLE 1.   Average Rank of Purchase Interest for Four Names for a New "Simpson" Mattress

Name	Average Rank of Purchase Intent [a] (from Scores on 100-point Purchase Intent Scale)	Base
SlumberJack	183	(50)
SlumberJack by Simpson	102	(50)
Sleepwell by Simpson	92	(50)
Sleepwell	86	(50)

Kruskal-Wallis test:
H = 9.7, χ^2 = 7.8 (df 3, P < .05)
Differences in average ranks for names significant: P < .05

[a] Ranks inverted so that higher average rank means stronger, more favorable, purchase intent.

TABLE 2. Comparisons of Purchase Intent Ranks for Four Names for a New "Simpson" Mattress [a]

Product Name	Sleepwell 88	Sleepwell by Simpson 90	SlumberJack by Simpson 99	SlumberJack 192	d	d-1	Z Table
Sleepwell (88)		-2.12	-2.52	-3.68	4	3	1.82
Sleepwell by Simpson (90)			-2.33	-3.76	3	2	2.78
SlumberJack by Simpson (99)				-3.21	2	1	2.35
SlumberJack							

[a] Ryan's procedure:
   Rank sum Zs entered in body of table must exceed Z tabled for comparison to be significant.
These significant differences occur:
   Sleepwell versus SlumberJack. $P < .05$.
   Sleepwell by Simpson versus SlumberJack. $P < .05$.
   SlumberJack by Simpson versus SlumberJack, $P < .05$

TABLE 3.   Reasons for Positive and Negative Purchase Intent

Purchase Intent	Percentage			
	SlumberJack	SlumberJack by Simpson	Sleepwell by Simpson	Sleepwell
Positive				
Gives a good night's sleep	16	7	5	16
Comfort	2	1	—	4
Softness	6	4	9	1
Firmness	—	1	5	—
Like the company's products	—	—	1	4
Would buy if needed	2	4	—	1
All respondents giving positive purchase intent	24	16	16	21
Negative				
No different from other brands	16	16	13	14
No better than current mattress	2	13	6	10
Don't like firmness	10	10	7	6
Not convincing or not appealing	4	4	5	7
Hard to believe claims	1	1	1	—
Dislike company's products	—	2	—	2
Never heard of it or won't try it	6	1	1	4
I don't need it	4	4	10	6
All respondents giving negative reasons	50	56	46	55
Base	(50)	(50)	(50)	(50)

The risk of introducing new products or line extensions is considerable. Product concept viability research helps to estimate whether trial levels will be good enough to go forward. Such research also gives an understanding of what the new entry will do to existing brands in the marketplace. This becomes much clearer when product quality information is added to what's known.

TECHNICAL APPENDIX

ALTERNATE DESIGNS FOR PRODUCT CONCEPT VIABILITY RESEARCH

Design Alternatives	Notes
Unit of analysis Category user Category purchaser Company brand user Company brand purchaser	Generally, category purchasers are sampled. When a product is being repositioned or a line extension is under consideration, company brand purchasers are involved usually.
Data collection Personal Telephone Mail	Personal is most frequent. When illustrated matter is used to present the product concept, mail remains a possibility. Personal is best for more complex designs.
Stimulus presentation Brand unidentified Brand identified	Concepts often have no brand name. When there is no name reaction to the product, idea is uncontaminated by a poor name. When a name is considered integral to the concept, it is part of the stimulus.
Consumer response Monadic Repeat	Repeat measures are used when a control is in the study. Single measures are used when there is normative history.
Evaluation criteria Competitor brands Company brand	Competitor brands are the usual standard. Sometimes a subjective expectation of response levels suffices. Sometimes norms from previous concept tests are used

ANALYTICAL TECHNIQUES

This section covers simple and specialized techniques that predict only a single, dependent variable. The specific techniques discussed are completely randomized analysis of variance (ANOVA) designs; randomized blocks (repeated measures ANOVA); split-plot (between-within ANOVA); and Kruskal-Wallis (an ANOVA analogue). These are among the simplest designs in the analysis of variance and related techniques. All analyses of variance test significances of differences between means: these analyses rely on several assumptions, including normal distributions and equal variances. Techniques discussed in this section have few variables and require only the most basic experimental conditions.

Completely Randomized Design, ANOVA

The completely randomized design tests the significance of differences between several independent groups on one dependent variable (that is at least an interval measure).

Each respondent is measured a single time only on this dependent variable. You may recognize this design by its "trade label": "monadic testing." For example, a manufacturer might consider four different names for a candy product. With the completely randomized design, each name would be exposed to one group of prospects only. The responses of each group would then be compared and tested.

The output of this analysis would include an F ratio. The F ratio signals the degree of difference between the means; it tells the likelihood that there are true differences between means rather than differences resulting from sampling fluctuations. The F ratio measure is fundamental to every analysis of variance design.

Analysis 5.1. "Commence" Car Batteries

In Case 5.1, Commence, three car battery concepts were tested using a completely randomized design (ANOVA). Variation due to the concepts was found to exceed an "experimental error" benchmark by a wide margin; this produced a high F ratio associated with a high significance level. The experiment was found to be sensitive; that is there were real differences between the concepts. A comparison test of means for the three concepts showed one concept the clear winner and no significant difference between the two losing concepts.

Randomized Blocks: Repeat Measures ANOVA

This design differs from the completely randomized ANOVA in that several measures of effect are obtained for each respondent. Repeat measures (within) designs are often labeled by researchers as "sequential designs." An example of these designs is this: a single group of prospects is asked to rate a half-dozen watch designs on a buying interest scale.

The use of a randomized blocks repeat measure design is intended to increase the efficiency of the study; fewer subjects are needed to determine significant differences. But such a study runs the risk of producing "carry over effects." *Carry over effects* are response biases that have been conditioned by previous exposure to experimental stimuli. You, the researcher, try to minimize such carry over effects by randomizing the order of concept presentation for each respondent.

Analysis 5.2. "CVC" Television

In Case 5.2, CVC Television, a new concept for a television set, Radio-Vision, was tested against a standard TV set control. A randomized blocks repeat measure ANOVA was performed. Both concepts were exposed to all respondents. A low F ratio was obtained, and the difference between test and control concepts was found not to be significant.

Split-Plot: Between-Within ANOVA

The split-plot, between-within ANOVA involves two independent variables—between and within groups, respectively. On one factor, each respondent is exposed to all levels or conditions. Individual respondents are assigned to only one level for the other factor. Suppose two lawn-mower models, regular and deluxe, are exposed to consumers. If management feels that the segments that are upper and lower income might differ in their responses to these models, a split-plot design might be suggested by the researcher. The design might call for balancing the sample into subsamples of lower and higher income. Then each subsample would be exposed to both lawn mowers.

The reason for using a split-plot is to block out some potentially serious sources of bias to learn how response to treatments (concepts) varies for specific groups. This leads to the idea of "interaction effects." Interaction effects occur when the effect of one variable is related to a particular level for the other variable. This is illustrated in Figure 5.1.

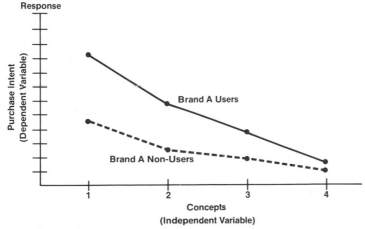

Figure 5.1.   An interaction between concepts and use (or nonuse) of brand A.

In this illustration, concepts are displayed on the horizontal axis and purchase intent on the vertical axis. The response of purchase intent to each of the concepts is shown separately for brand A users and for brand A nonusers. It is apparent from the chart that the difference in response between the two brand-use segments varies with the particular concept examined. Therefore, an example of an interaction effect is being illustrated. The chart also shows that the relative ranks of the concepts on the response variable (purchase intent) are the same for each segment. Therefore, the analysis also would show a significant "main effect"—that is, a general tendency for one or more concepts to differ from others, regardless of the user segment involved.

Analysis 5.3. "Stratford" Sewing Machines

In Case 5.3, Stratford, each respondent was exposed in random order to eight concepts (all concepts tested). This represents the between aspect of the analysis. In addition, each respondent was classified as either a beginner or an experienced sewer—segments regarded as having potential marketing importance. This represented the within part of the analysis. The main effect of the concepts was found to be significant, and the interaction of concepts and experience level was not. The test showed that concepts significantly affect purchase intent response. A single concept emerged as stronger than all others on purchase intent, based on a subsequent comparison test.

Kruskal-Wallis Test

Return, for a moment, to the simple randomized design, ANOVA. The same basic type of design may be analyzed in an analogous but different way. If assumptions for a standard analysis of variance are "shaky" for the study data, you, the researcher, may want to use a more conservative technique—even if the latter is less sensitive for a given sample size. Another reason for using an analog rather than the standard ANOVA is that the dependent variable may be less than interval measurement.

One analog for ANOVA is the Kruskal-Wallis test, a nonparametric technique for testing significance. This test assumes only that samples must be random and independent and are drawn from an underlying continuous distribution. An "H Statistic" is derived in this test. The H Statistic is based on totals for ranks of each group, when all respondents have been pooled and ranks assigned.

Analysis 5.4. A New "Simpson" Mattress Line

In Case 5.4, Simpson, test data appeared not to be drawn from a normal population. The researcher decided to look at differences in responses to four names for a line extension (among four independent groups). A Kruskal-Wallis test was used to probe for significance. Data were "reduced" from interval to ranked. The results were found to contain "true" differences. A single name emerged as strongest when a comparison test appropriate to ranked data and a completely randomized design was done.

COMPUTER ANALYSIS

A numerical example of the completely randomized ANOVA is presented in this section. The purpose of the analysis is to ascertain whether differences between the means of several independent groups are true or are the result of random variation.

Analysis Plan: Completely Randomized ANOVA

Each respondent is measured once and for one treatment (i.e., level) only. There is one independent, nominal variable, B, with four levels. The dependent variable, RESPONSE, is interval scaled from 1 to 11. Table 5.1 shows that B's levels have been assigned values of 1, 2, 3, 4—subscripts of treatments (line 1). Also shown is the respondent sample size, $n = 32$ (line 2).

Computer Output

Table 5.2 shows the analysis of variance for the dependent variable, RESPONSE. On line 1, "degrees of freedom," (df) are shown for each source of variance. *Degrees of freedom* are a numerical descriptive measure of the F ratio distribution used to test significance in this analysis. Sum of squares and mean square are shown. The latter is the ratio of squares and degrees of freedom. R^2 is an index, from 0 to 1, that shows the degree to which the model fits the data. C.V. stands for coefficient of variation and indicates the amount of population variance.

TABLE 5.1. Completely Randomized Anova

COMPLETELY RANDOMIZED ANOVA (SAS BATCH)

ANALYSIS OF VARIANCE PROCEDURE

CLASS LEVEL INFORMATION

	CLASS	LEVELS	VALUES
1			
	B	4	1 2 3 4
2	NUMBER OF OBSERVATIONS IN DATA SET = 32		

TABLE 5.2.   Completely Randomized Anova

COMPLETELY RANDOMIZED ANOVA (SAS BATCH)

ANALYSI

DEPENDENT VARIABLE: RESPONSE

	SOURCE	DF	SUM OF SQUARES
1			
	MODEL	3	143.59375000
2	ERROR	28	62.37500000
	CORRECTED TOTAL	31	205.96875000
3	SOURCE	DF	ANOVA SS
	B	3	143.59375000

Line 2 refers to the error (residual) source of variation and the standard deviation (SD) of the dependent variable, as well as its mean.

Line 3 indicates, for the measured source of variance, the F ratio for use in testing the problem hypothesis. The probability associated with the F ratio for its degrees of freedom also is displayed.

Interpretation

The analysis of Table 5.2 tests the significance of the differences in the treatment means for the four levels of variable B. The significance level ($PR - F$) is shown as 0.0001, indicative of a reliable difference. The significance traces from $F = 21.49$, df $= 3$. The R^2 value, 0.697163, confirms that the model explains much of the variation in variable RESPONSE.

VARIANCE PROCEDURE

MEAN SQUARE	F VALUE	PR > F	R-SQUARE	C.V.
47.86458333	21.49	0.0001	0.697163	26.9838
2.22767857		STD DEV		RESPONSE MEAN
		1.49254098		5.53125000

VALUE	PR > F
21.49	0.0001

SIX

Product Performance

Quality of product performance determines how many of a brand's customers will continue to buy a product after their first purchase. Therefore, you, the researcher, are asked to measure and evaluate performance of your company's or client's products.

Product performance refers to consumers' after-use, overall product ratings and their ratings for specific product characteristics. Examples of such characteristics are "foaming action" for a household cleanser or "oven size" for an electric range.

In Chapter 3, I presented problems and research techniques relating to product concepts. In this chapter, marketing problems relate to the ways consumers feel about products they actually use. Further, I show how research is designed to measure these feelings. Now, let's see the contribution you, the researcher, make by doing product performance studies.

Assure good product performance; relate claims to products. Before a product is finally marketed, product performance research measures the product's acceptability to consumers. This is the case whether the concern is with replacing a product currently on the market or introducing a new one. For a product to succeed, it should perform well in comparison to its competition.

The research you conduct shows how well claims match with a product's performance. You may present claims to consumers, and then see if the product satisfies these claims. On the other hand, you may have consumers try a product first—to discover which claims make the most sense to them.

You control product quality and make claims and products harmonize by doing a variety of product performance studies. Exhibit 6.1 shows product performance research problems with which you deal. Each problem concerns product acceptance from a different point of view. Let's examine the first of these—when consumers rate acceptability using their own criteria in the early stages of product development.

EXHIBIT 6.1.   Examples of Product Performance Problems

Research Problems	Primary Aim
Guiding product development	Determine acceptable formulation levels
Deciding to change products	Improve acceptance of existing products
Making new product quality competitive	Outperform competitors in product acceptance
Having products deliver what they promise	Reinforce product acceptance

GUIDING PRODUCT DEVELOPMENT

Product development work goes ahead only when the range of acceptable formulations is known. Products must meet set qualifications before full-scale performance testing.

Formula guidance research provides early screening and assists development of rough formulations. The product manager searches for products that are very good performers. Often she or he wants products that meet basic criteria for new concepts or are good enough to replace existing ones.

A variety of products are tested in sequence in formula guidance work. Results of earlier tests provide direction to develop products to be used in later tests. The cycle continues as formulations approach an acceptable range for consumer satisfaction. Formula guidance activity ends when one or more formulations meet marketing's product performance standards. Consumer research at the earliest stages of product development provides safeguards that assure basic levels of product quality.

Case Preview: "Vita Punch" Soft Drink

Case 6.1, Vita Punch, illustrates the role research plays in determining the risk associated with a substitute ingredient for an established brand. The Research and Development department had produced a new formulation for Vita Punch by substituting sucrose for dextrose; this substitution represented a substantial potential savings in product costs. The researcher recommended to Marketing that a product placement study of the modified product be conducted. The study was conducted to determine how the product with sucrose performed among loyal Vita Punch users, especially on a perceived energy benefit, relative to the current product with dextrose.

Marketers of Vita Punch favored the substitution, primarily because of the potential cost savings. However, they were afraid of the risk of introducing an inferior product. They were anxious to learn how the product with sucrose performed relative to the current product. Research and Development prepared two batches of test products (one with sucrose and one with dextrose) for placement and the fieldwork began.

Based on product performance scores, the research report recommended the introduction of the product with sucrose in place of dextrose. The research illustrated that the cost savings associated with a product substitution can be especially profitable when the reformulated product performs as well as the current product among loyal brand users.

Case 6.1 "Vita Punch" Soft Drink Formula Guidance Research

Objective

Research and Development has produced a new formulation of Vita Punch. This new formulation substitutes sucrose for the dextrose that is contained in the product now on the market. Based on recent market prices for dextrose, the substitution of sucrose could result in an annual savings of approximately $60,000 for Vita Punch, on the basis of the current standard cost (Marketing's estimate).

The objective of this test is to provide an estimate of the opportunity and risk in a go/no-go decision for Vita Punch with sucrose. If results are favorable for the new ingredient, Research and Development will continue formula guidance work on the sucrose product. The purpose of continuing developmental work, if warranted, is to find the most advantageous levels of the ingredient, as measured in sequential tests.

This study provides an informational basis for a decision to substitute or not to substitute sucrose for dextrose on a national basis.

Method

The objective was met by conducting a product placement test among department store employees. Data collection took place while employees were on a coffee break in the store.

This test was conducted among two groups of respondents, designated as sucrose and dextrose. A quota was set for each group of respondents on the basis of sex, age, and first-time user status. Participants in both groups were told to sip two ounces of water prior to the test to clear their taste buds. Meanwhile, the interviewer premeasured Vita Punch in a clear plastic cup with a liquid measure printed outside. Then the interviewer gave the respondent the Vita Punch to drink and waited for the respondent to finish drinking the sample. Fifty interviews were completed per group.

Research made its recommendation about whether to proceed with the substitution of the new formulation of Vita Punch, based on how the two products performed on the key measure: perceived energy. It was agreed that the ingredient change required that the sucrose product perform as well as the dextrose product on this measure.

A completely randomized factorial, two-way analysis of variance was used to measure the significance of the observed mean differences in perceived energy for the two formulations and for the sex of the users.

Recommendations and Conclusions

The new formulation is recommended as a substitute for the current Vita Punch formulation. Overall, the new formulation of Vita Punch scores on par with the current formulation on the perceived energy measure; the analysis of variance shows no difference overall. A significant difference is found in favor of sucrose among women users of Vita Punch. It is concluded that little risk would be assumed by substituting the new formulation for the current formulation. See Tables 1–3.

There is little difference between the new formulation and the current formulation in terms of such attributes as taste, aroma, and color. See Tables 4–6.

The new formulation scores slightly (but not significantly) above the current formulation on purchase intent. See Table 7.

TABLE 1.   Average Perceived Energy Rating for the New Sucrose Formulation and the Current Dextrose Formulation of "Vita Punch" (by Sex—5-Point Scale)

	"Vita Punch" Formulation	
Sex	Sucrose	Dextrose
Women	3.55	3.33
Men	3.41	3.37
Total	3.48	3.35

TABLE 2.   Sources of Variation in Purchase Allocation for "Vita Punch" Formulations

Sources of Variation	MS=Mean Square	F	df	Significance Level
Formulation	17.14	2.98	1	N.S.
Sex	16.04	2.79	1	N.S.
Formulation × Sex	30.82	5.36	1	$P < .05$
Error	5.75		96	
Total			99	

ი

TABLE 3.   Rating of Perceived Energy from the New Formulation and from the Current Product

Rating	Percentage According to "Vita Punch" Formulation	
	Sucrose	Dextrose
Excellent	13	13
Very good	36	26
Good	38	45
Fair	13	16
Poor	—	—
Total	100	100
Base	(50)	(50)
Mean[a]	3.48	3.35

Question: Now would you tell me how you rate Vita Punch on several characteristics using the ratings excellent, very good, good, fair, or poor?

[a] Based on scaled rating: 1 (for poor) to 5 (for excellent).

TABLE 4.   Rating of the Taste of the New Formulation and of the Current Product

Rating	Percentage According to "Vita Punch" Formulation	
	Sucrose	Dextrose
Excellent	7	—
Very good	16	19
Good	48	62
Fair	13	16
Poor	16	3
Total	100	100
Base	(50)	(50)
Mean[a]	2.84	2.97

Question: Now would you tell me how you rate Vita Punch on several characteristics using the ratings excellent, very good, good, fair, or poor?

[a] Based on scaled rating: 1 (for poor) to 5 (for excellent).

DECIDING TO CHANGE PRODUCTS

When brand loyalty falls off, a product's quality becomes suspect. Then companies are faced with the problem of confirming whether a reformulation strategy is sound. Assuming a reformulation strategy is sound, there is the further problem of what to do about it.

Product performance studies can test consumer acceptance of products designed to replace existing ones. A replacement product is recommended for

TABLE 5.   Rating of the Aroma of the New Formulation and of the Current Product

	Percentage According to "Vita Punch" Formulation	
Rating	Sucrose	Dextrose
Excellent	13	—
Very good	13	19
Good	42	52
Fair	22	26
Poor	10	3
Total	100	100
Base	(50)	(50)
Mean [a]	2.97	2.87

Question: Now would you tell me how you rate Vita Punch on several characteristics using the ratings excellent, very good, good, fair, or poor?

[a] Based on scaled rating: 1 (for poor) to 5 (for excellent).

TABLE 6.   Rating of the Color of the New Formulation and of the Current Product

	Percentage According to "Vita Punch" Formulation	
Rating	Sucrose	Dextrose
Excellent	7	—
Very good	10	10
Good	54	74
Fair	26	16
Poor	3	—
Total	100	100
Base	(50)	(50)
Mean [a]	2.90	2.94

Question: Now would you tell me how you rate Vita Punch on several characteristics using the ratings excellent, very good, good, fair, or poor?

[a] Based on scaled rating: 1 (for poor) to 5 (for excellent).

marketplace introduction when research shows it performs well in comparison to the current product. In some cases, a replacement product is expected to be indistinguishable from the current product. This happens, for example, when the current product's performance is very satisfactory but ingredient problems make reformulation necessary.

Product performance testing can diagnose weaknesses in existing products. The direction for product reformulation is given when product weaknesses are found.

TABLE 7.   Rating of the Purchase Intent of the New Formulation and of the Current Product

Purchase Intent	Percentage According to "Vita Punch" Formulation	
	Sucrose	Dextrose
Definitely buy	48	42
Probably buy	32	35
Might or might not buy	10	—
Probably would not buy	7	10
Definitely would not buy	3	13
Total	100	100
Base	(50)	(50)
Mean [a]	4.16	3.84

Question: Suppose Vita Punch were available in stores; which of the following statements best express how likely you would be to buy Vita Punch?

[a] Based on scaled rating: 1 (for "definitely would not buy") to 5 (for "definitely would buy").

Product reformulation is considered by the product manager for one or more of these reasons: (1) learn if the product needs improvement, (2) turn around a poor sales trend, (3) protect against vulnerabilities to competitive products, (4) increase customer satisfaction and loyalty, (5) heighten awareness of the product and benefits, (6) control costs when ingredient prices rise, and (7) assure distribution when there is a supply problem with raw materials.

Reformulation may lead to dramatic improvements in product performance. In such cases, it is common to call attention to the improvement on product packaging and elsewhere. By strengthening claims, it is easier to attract and hold customers.

Case Preview: "Perma-Mist" Hair Spray

Case 6.2, Perma-Mist, stemmed from work by the Research and Development department in an attempt to reformulate a product. The department had produced two new Perma-Mist hair spray prototypes. One of these was expected to replace the current aerosol-type hair spray. Research was asked to design a study that measured the actual performance of each of these prototypes. The study's aim was to determine the marketability of each of these brands relative to a competitive brand.

The researcher and Marketing conferred about several of the research issues—such as which competitive brand would be used as a control—and details concerning the length of time to place products.

The research conclusions stated that a wide valve prototype was recommended over one with a narrow valve for in-market distribution. The conclusion was based on the wide valve prototype's allocation score. The narrow valve was acceptable as an interim product until the wide valve became available.

The research illustrated that although one of the test reformulations may outscore another they both can be acceptable and useful as reformulations of a current brand.

Case 6.2   "Perma-Mist" Hair Spray Product Modification or Replacement Test

Objective

The F.D.A. and various consumer groups have criticized the noxious effects of aerosol gaseous inhalation. Such criticism has appeared in national print.

Of the pump hair spray prototypes, two Perma-Mist nonaerosols have been produced by Research and Development. Each pump spray is designed to provide the following advantages:

It does not produce a lingering mist; consequently it is safer to use.

Exceeds the usual triammonium chloride nonoxynol content found in most aerosols by four to five times. The result is greater efficiency for the pump spray, with respect to deposit of ingredients on hair.

It is more economical to use on a per application basis.

The prototype pump sprays are identical in every way (including size), except for the valve that differs between one pump prototype (Narrow Valve) and the other prototype (Wide Valve).

The objective of this research is to compare the actual performance of each Perma-Mist pump spray product against that of a control product, Brand X; measure strengths and weaknesses; and determine the marketability of each pump spray.

Method

A total of 220 respondents who currently use hair spray at least three times per week were contacted by means of a shopping center intercept. The test and control products were subsequently used by 200 respondents who tried the product for one week. Placement was on a blind basis.

The pump spray with the highest purchase allocation was to be recommended for further development.

Recommendations and Conclusions

Perma-Mist's Wide Valve Pump Spray is recommended over Narrow Valve Pump Spray for in-market distribution on the basis of its higher purchase allocation score. Narrow Valve, however, is acceptable as an interim in-market substitute for Wide Valve, since Narrow Valve has a sufficiently strong purchase allocation score.

The Perma-Mist Wide Valve Pump Spray outperforms Brand X hair spray—an established leader in the field and an aerosol—and therefore is considered a strong entry for market introduction. Although the Narrow Valve Pump Spray does not perform as well as Wide Valve Pump Spray in purchase allocation, it does perform on a par with Brand X; hence Research recommends Narrow Valve Pump Spray for interim use in the event that Wide Valve is in short supply.

The analysis of variance test used shows Wide Valve Pump Spray's superiority to Narrow Valve. A significant interaction is found between test pump sprays and hair length. Further analysis of this interaction shows that women with short hair favor Wide Valve even more strongly than do the other women. The main effects for brand use and hair length are significant; this indicates that the design for the analysis of variance has selected significant variables. See Tables 1 and 2.

TABLE 1.   Average Purchase Aiiocation for Two Types of "Perma-Mist" Pump Sprays (by Competitive Brands and Hair Length — 10 Points Divided between Test Pump Spray and Brand X)

Brand Used	Hair Length	Wide Valve Pump Spray	Narrow Valve Pump Spray
Brand X	Short	5.85	4.53
	Medium	5.15	4.42
	Long	5.01	4.31
Other brands	Short	7.96	6.31
	Medium	6.21	5.30
	Long	6.17	5.27
Total		6.06	5.02

TABLE 2.   Sources of Variation in Purchase Allocation for Two Pump Spray Systems for "Perma-Mist" Hair Spray

Sources of Variation	MS=Mean Square	F	df	Significance Level
Competitive brand	23.55	5.66	1	$P < .05$
Pump sprays	22.13	5.32	1	$P < .05$
Hair length	8.49	2.04	2	N.S.
Competitive brand × Pump sprays	4.70	1.13	1	N.S.
Competitive brand × Hair length	5.16	1.24	2	N.S.
Pump sprays × Hair length	17.93	4.31	2	$P < .05$
Competitive brand × Pump sprays × Hair length	9.86	2.37	2	N.S.
Error	4.16		188	
Total			199	

Product safety and lack of a lingering mist are strong points of favorable difference. Respondents in this test—aerosol hair spray users—generally like the idea of a pump hair spray for safety reasons and because it doesn't have a lingering mist. Respondents rate it higher than aerosols on these attributes. The pump spray delivers a variety of end benefits on about the same high level reported for the aerosol tested.

There are a few weak performance areas for Wide Valve (possibly inherent in the pump spray technology). The product delivered is wetter and less even in application than is an aerosol. Communications for the brand should avoid any suggestion that the product goes on dry. See Table 3.

At the conclusion of the interview, respondents were asked how they felt about having a pump hair spray, such as the one they tried, available for purchase. In general, respondents from both subsamples (who currently use an

TABLE 3. Overall Product Satisfaction and Rating on Specific Product Qualities (between Two Products Tested)

Product Qualities	Wide Valve	vs.	Brand X Hair Spray	Narrow Valve	vs.	Brand X Hair Spray
Product satisfaction	7.4		7.4	7.2		7.5
Is safe to use	9.7		7.5	9.2		7.5
Seems to last long	9.5		9.1	9.8		8.5
It's not irritating	9.1		9.5	8.8		9.4
Helps hold hair in place	9.0		8.7	9.2		8.5
Spray mist does not linger	9.0		7.5	9.1		6.7
Is not sticky	8.9		8.8	9.6		9.0
Like appearance of container	8.8		7.9	8.8		7.6
Leaves hair looking natural	8.7		8.4	9.1		8.3
Goes on evenly	8.3		9.6	7.8		9.4
Spray works well	8.2		10.0	8.7		9.9
Has a pleasant scent	8.2		8.0	8.0		7.4
Goes on dry	6.0		7.4	5.5		6.5
Base		(100)			(100)	

Question: On a scale of 1–11, with 11 being remarkably good and 1 being extremely poor, how would you rate the hair spray product you tried second on providing overall product satisfaction? In other words, the higher the number, the better the product was in providing overall product satisfaction; the lower the number, the worse the product was on providing overall satisfaction. Do you understand this scale of 1–11?

Now, I would like your opinion of the product you just tried in terms of a few specific qualities. I will read a statement to you; then I want you to rate the product you just tried for that quality using the same scale of 1–11, with 11 being remarkably good and 1 being extremely poor.

TABLE 4. Feelings about Having Hair Spray Pump Available

Reactions	Wide Valve vs. Brand X Hair Spray (%)	Narrow Valve vs. Brand X Hair Spray (%)
Positive		
Pump Applicator (net)	48	38
Easy to use or handle convenient	32	12
Like the applicator or pump spray	12	10
Covers well	6	6
Like the fine mist	4	10
Not shocking cold	2	10
All other pump applicator mentions	16	8
Health or safety (net)	26	24
No fumes in the air	12	14
Safer or not dangerous	12	4
Not detrimental to atmosphere	8	—
No fumes to irritate lungs or nose	4	2
All other health or safety mentions	—	4
Miscellaneous positive		
I like it, or it's very good	40	36
It's a good idea or good replacement for aerosols	22	16
I would buy it	14	18
Effective or works for me	12	16
Better than or as good as aerosols	10	14
All other miscellaneous positive	12	4
Miscellaneous neutral		
I would buy it if the product was good or effective	8	14
I would buy it if they improved the application	8	2
It's okay, fair, pretty good	2	10
I would buy it if the price were right	2	4
All other neutral mentions	2	8

TABLE 4. *(cont'd)*

Reactions	Wide Valve vs.	Brand X Hair Spray (%)	Narrow Valve vs.	Brand X Hair Spray (%)
Negative				
Pump applicator (net)		28		34
Messy		18		10
Wet, runny, drippy		16		16
Harder to use or manipulate		10		8
Inconvenient		4		4
Doesn't spray as well		2		10
All other application mentions		—		10
Miscellaneous negative				
Wouldn't buy it or don't like it		16		22
Too big or clumsy		6		2
All other miscellaneous negative		6		4
Base		(100)		(100)

Question: And, finally, how do you feel in general about having a hair spray pump, such as the one you tried, available for purchase at your local store?

aerosol hair spray product on a regular basis) are favorable about the future availability of a pump spray. See Table 4.

MAKING NEW PRODUCT QUALITY COMPETITIVE

Even if new product concepts are so appealing that there is widespread trial, problems remain. How do you as the researcher select new entry products that perform well enough to stay in the marketplace?

Product performance research helps select new entry product designs. The studies you conduct tell how well products deliver benefits in the brand's plan. They provide evidence for cases in which the new entry products are demonstrably superior to their competitors.

If the evidence is compelling, a product can be advertised or promoted with specific claims of product superiority. If performance of the new entry product is exceptionally good, a sampling program may be included in the market introduction stage.

Product performance studies also provide disaster checks against the possibility of a new entry product weakness that is unexpected and serious. An example might be a bath oil that does a fine job of skin softening but begins to look unsightly in its bottle. Research can indicate that a new entry product will satisfy consumers only in the short run—as a fad. Such information will lead to revision or even shelving of the marketing plan.

Case Preview: "Carry Kleen" Hand Cleanser

Case 6.3, Carry Kleen, describes a new product performance study in which another of the company's hand cleansers served as the control for evaluating its hand cleansing Towelettes. The control product was different in form but similar in function.

Marketers felt confident about the performance of the new Towelettes. Nevertheless, they wanted a concrete measure of consumers' evaluations of the performance of Towelettes. Marketing was especially interested in the analysis of the data by occupational class and regular product form. These two variables were expected to condition responses to the product. Marketing and the researcher discussed these information needs with the researcher and agreed on a study design.

The researcher recommended further development of the Towelettes. The data indicated that the two variables mentioned previously did influence product performance.

Case 6.3 "Carry Kleen" Hand Cleanser New Product Test

Objective

Marketing is considering the introduction of a product. The proposed entry is a Towelettes product that is used as a hand cleanser. The Towelettes would be dispensed individually from a container designed to keep the Towelettes moist. The dispensed Towelettes are large. Presumably, they are as efficacious as the current solvent product that the company markets.

The primary objective of this research is to determine whether this Towelettes prototype is sufficiently strong in performance to be considered for the next level of marketing development.

Method

A panel of 240 males was recruited. The panel was subdivided into four equal cells of 60 respondents each. The cells consisted of white-collar or blue-collar recent users of solvent or liquid soap. Each respondent was asked to use the Towelettes prototype, identified by brand. Additionally, all respondents in this study, on a rotating basis, received an identified control product—the company's regular solvent product.*

*The Towelettes prototype was identified as Carry Kleen Towelettes; the solvent product was identified as it is in its regular packaging.

It was expected that occupational class and the regular product form would condition responses to the Carry Kleen Towelette and its solvent control. Accordingly, each respondent who used both the test Towelettes and test solvent (in randomly assigned order) was assigned randomly to one of four independent cells. Each cell represented a specific occupational class, combined with a specific form of hand cleanser used as the regular product.

Recommendations and Conclusions

Carry Kleen Towelettes prototype product is recommended for the next level of marketing development. There are no data available from this limited test or prior research regarding the level of acceptance for the Towelettes concept. Research recommends concept acceptance and concept placement testing early in the product's market development. This kind of testing might also deal with the question of whether the Towelettes should be marketed as (1) a line extension of the solvent, (2) a line extension of the brand, or (3) an entirely new product.

Relative to the solvent control product, Towelettes achieve at least parity among solvent users, based on an overall performance rating score.

Overall means for the tested Towelettes and solvent are virtually the same. The lack of significant difference between the two products tested is validated in a split-plot, between-between-within analysis of variance. Significant interaction effects are found that indicate the following: (1) white-collar workers are more likely to be receptive to the tested Towelettes than they are to the solvent, and the reverse is true for blue-collar workers; (2) the most receptive to the tested Towelettes are white-collar workers whose regular product is the solvent.

When occupation is not explicitly considered, reaction to each of the products tested appears unrelated to the regular product used (interaction between the regular product and the product tested is not significant). See Tables 1–4.

The primary qualities liked about Towelettes product include "cleans

TABLE 1. Average Overall Ratings for Towelettes and Solvent Hand Cleansers (by Occupational Class and Regular Cleanser Product Form)

Occupational Class	Regular Product	Product Tested (11-Point Scale)	
		Towelettes	Solvents
White-collar	Solvent	10.6	10.2
workers	Liquid soap	8.4	7.8
Blue-collar	Solvent	9.6	10.6
workers	Liquid soap	9.3	9.2
Total ($n = 240$)		9.5	9.6

TABLE 2. Average Overall Ratings for Towelettes and Solvent Hand Cleansers (by Regular Hand Cleanser Product Form)

Regular Product	Product Tested (11-Point Scale)	
	Towelettes	Solvents
Solvent	10.1	10.4
Soap	8.8	8.5
Total	9.5	9.6

TABLE 3. Average Overall Ratings for Towelettes and Solvent Hand Cleansers (by Occupational Class)

Occupational Class	Product Tested (11-Point Scale)	
	Towelettes	Solvent
White-collar workers	9.5	9.0
Blue-collar workers	9.5	9.9
Total	9.5	9.6

TABLE 4. Sources of Variation in Overall Ratings for Two Forms of Hand Cleansers

Sources of Variation	MS = Mean Square	F	df	Significance Level
Between respondents	—		239	
Occupation	4.42	3.30	1	N.S.
Regular product	9.73	7.26	1	$P < .01$
Occupation × regular product	4.19	3.13	1	N.S.
Error: between respondents	1.34		236	
Within respondents	—		240	
Products tested	3.04	2.69	1	N.S.
Occupation × products tested	5.10	4.51	1	$P < .05$
Regular product × products tested	3.18	2.81	1	N.S.
Occupation × regular product × product tested	5.48	4.85	1	$P < .05$
Error: within respondents	1.13		236	
Total			239	

112

thoroughly," "easy or convenient to use," and "doesn't dry out or stays wet." See Table 5.

There is some indication (from qualities disliked) that the Towelettes prototypes are hard to separate or difficult to get out of the packaging. See Table 6.

On a specific question about container size, the prototype is considered adequate by most of the consumers tested. See Table 7.

HAVING PRODUCTS DELIVER WHAT THEY PROMISE

Having a good product concept and a good performing product may not be enough to assure success. That is why you, the researcher, are often called on to study product performance among prospects who show interest in a concept.

Marketing programs are built around those concept and product combinations that offer the best and most inviting returns on effort. When the favorable concept-product combinations are identified, results can lead to further improvements. If there are suggested weaknesses in trial or repeat components of sales performance levels, these can be strengthened. For a line extension introduction, management is concerned about cannibalization of sales from existing products in the company's line. The research done by you tells what kind of marketplace impact to anticipate.

Thus benefits and risks associated with the planned introductions can be evaluated. In addition, these studies provide information to sharpen and improve plans for marketing new product entries.

Case Preview: "Silky" Hair Conditioner

Case 6.4, Silky, is a study in which purchase interest was measured for four variations of the same product (each variation offered one of four ingredients that was considered as an addition to one formulation). Research had determined that the product claim "untangles your hair" could be supported by the addition of any one of these four products. Marketing had to determine that the production costs would be approximately the same for the four ingredients. Research was requested to measure before-use attitudes toward these ingredients, as inputs to consumer purchase decisions.

The advertising agency created the product concepts used in this study. The research made use of packages bearing the brand name and the promoted product ingredient. The researcher coordinated the efforts of the involved departments. She made sure the fieldwork began as soon as possible.

Study results indicated that Silky Hair Conditioner with Panthenol outscored the three alternatives. Panthenol was recommended for market introduction. The research identified the target market for this product.

TABLE 5. Likes about Towelettes and Solvents (by Type of Hand Cleanser Used)

| | Total | | Regular Product | | | |
| | | | Solvent | | Soap | |
Qualities Liked	Tested Towelettes (%)	Tested Solvent (%)	Tested Towelettes (%)	Tested Solvent (%)	Tested Towelettes (%)	Tested Solvent (%)
Effectiveness						
Cleans thoroughly	50	59	6	11	8	7
Product is Effective; it does the job	32	32	3	6	6	4
Sanitary	11	23	2	5	1	2
Good for variety of occasions	9	9	2	1	2	3
Ease of use						
Easy or convenient to use	32	16	2	3	6	3
Easy to get out of container	23	7	2	1	5	2
Just discard when finished	7	—	—	—	—	—
Convenient when traveling	2	2	1	1	1	1
Easy to separate or tear	2	4	—	1	—	—
Can cover area you want to clean	2	—	—	—	1	—

Not messy					
Not messy to use	16	9	4	2	1
Doesn't drip	8	2	3	—	1
Doesn't get on clothes	4	—	—	1	—
Not sticky or gummy	2	7	1	1	—
Feel on skin					
Not rough to skin	11	4	2	—	—
feels pleasant	7	—	1	—	—
Doesn't irritate	4	4	1	—	—
Miscellaneous likes					
Doesn't dry out or stays wet	23	16	1	6	2
Used quickly	11	4	—	2	—
Towelettes, pads right; good size	7	2	1	1	1
Like container	5	9	1	1	—
Not dangerous like aerosol	5	—	—	2	—
Base	(240)	(120)	(120)	(120)	(120)

Question: What, if anything, did you particularly like about the product you tried?

115

TABLE 6. Dislikes about Towelettes and Solvents (by Type of Hand Cleanser Used)

| | Total | | Regular Product | | | |
| | | | Solvent | | Soap | |
Qualities Disliked	Tested Towelettes (%)	Tested Solvent (%)	Tested Towelettes (%)	Tested Solvent (%)	Tested Towelettes (%)	Tested Solvent (%)
Hard to use	36	23	7	2	4	4
Hard to separate or get out of jar	32	16	5	2	4	4
Don't like having to discard	6	8	2	—	1	—
Messy	27	39	1	2	3	8
Left hands messy	16	23	—	2	2	4
Sticky, gummy, greasy	6	9	1	—	1	3
Messy to handle	5	11	—	—	—	2
Degree of wetness	11	11	3	—	2	4
Too wet	9	9	2	—	2	3
Not wet enough	2	2	1	—	—	1
Effectiveness						
Doesn't clean well	4	4	1	—	1	2
Not effective	2	2	1	—	1	2

(general)	2	2	—	—	1
Miscellaneous dislikes					
Product too large	7	—	1	—	1
Takes too long to use	7	5	1	1	1
Don't like container	4	11	—	—	1
Skin broke out; irritated skin	2	2	—	—	—
Don't like the feel	2	2	—	1	—
Container too large	2	—	1	—	—
Not as good as regular brand or type	—	4	—	—	1
(Base)[a]	(240)	(120)		(120)	(120)

Question: What, if anything, did you particularly dislike about the product you tried?

[a]Totals to more than 100% because of multiple mentions.

117

TABLE 7. Reaction to Towelettes and Solvent Container Size (by Type of Hand Cleanser Regularly Used)

| | Total | | Regular Product | | | | | |
| | | | Solvent | | Soap | | | |
Reaction	Tested Towelettes (%)	Tested Solvent (%)	Tested Towelettes (%)	Tested Solvent (%)	Tested Towelettes (%)	Tested Solvent (%)
Adequate	89	84	11	12	14	13
Not adequate	11	16	3	2	1	2
Total	100	100				
(Base)	(240)		(120)		(120)	

Question: How do you feel about the size of the container? Would you say that the container used is adequate or——?

[a] Base too small to give a percentage.

118

Case 6.4   Consumer Evaluation of "Silky" Hair Conditioner

Objective

The Touchable Silk franchise is considering the introduction of a new hair conditioner. Previous concept research has indicated that a strong market opportunity exists for Silky Hair Conditioner. The brand is positioned especially for people with long hair—people whose hair is likely to be all tangled after it is washed.

Earlier research, "Formulation Guidance for Silky Hair Conditioner," has indicated that the claim "untangles your hair" can be supported to about the same extent by the addition of any one of four ingredients—panthenol, protein, balsam, or henna. Therefore, the choice of the "lead" ingredient for the product will depend on consumer before-use response to each of these ingredients.

The primary purpose of this research is to determine which one ingredient would have the most potential sales vitality for Silky Hair Conditioner's introduction.

Method

Respondents were contacted by means of a shopping center intercept. Personal interviews were conducted with 120 respondents (60 in each of the two markets) in different geographic regions. The sample consisted of women, 18 years or older, who were aware of the Touchable Silk franchise name (unaided and aided).

All respondents were first exposed to the basic Silky Hair Conditioner concept. Each respondent was exposed simultaneously, in random order, to all four Silky ingredients. Each ingredient was displayed prominently on a package bearing the brand name logos. Respondents were asked to rate each product before them on purchase interest, using a 100-point scale. This scale was labeled "Definitely would buy," alongside 80−100; "Probably would buy," alongside 60−79; down to "Definitely would not buy," alongside 0−19.

The recommendation about the best ingredient to feature for Silky used the 100-point purchase interest scale measure as a criterion.

Examination of the raw data and individual cases strongly suggested that respondents were actually going through a ranking procedure rather than a rating procedure—that each ingredient tended to be placed into an ordered class.

Since there were strong doubts about the earlier assumptions of interval measurement, it was decided to make use of the Friedman test, a nonparametric procedure.

Recommendations and Conclusions

Silky Hair Conditioner with Panthenol outscores other alternatives on the decision criterion. The proposed entry item, therefore, is recommended for introduction. The scores generated by the panthenol ingredient surpass scores for protein, balsam, and henna on the purchase interest criterion. The Friedman test shows that the average ranks for the four alternative ingredients differ significantly. A Nemenyi's comparison test for differences in mean ranks shows that panthenol is clearly superior to all other ingredients in generating purchase interest for Silky Hair Conditioner. It should be noted that this same test shows henna to be an extremely weak entry—consistent with marketing intelligence that hair products featuring this ingredient are experiencing a downtrend. See Tables 1 and 2.

TABLE 1.   Average Rank of Purchase Interest for Four Ingredient Features for "Silky" Hair Conditioner

Ingredient	Average Rank of Purchase Intent (From Scores on a 10-point Purchase Intent Scale) [a]
Panthenol	62
Protein	51
Balsam	48
Henna	29
Base	(120)

Friedman test:
$X^r = X^2 = 10.89$ (df 3, $P<.05$)
Differences in average ranks for ingredients significant:
$P < .05$

[a] Ranks inverted so that higher average rank means a stronger, more favorable purchase intent.

TABLE 2.   Comparisons of Purchase Intent Ranks for Four Ingredient Features for "Silky" Hair Conditioner

Ingredient	Panthenol $\overline{X}$ 62	Protein $\overline{X}$ 51	Balsam $\overline{X}$ 48	Henna $\overline{X}$ 29
Panthenol $\overline{X}$ 62	—	11 [a]	14 [a]	33 [a]
Protein $\overline{X}$ 51		—	3	22 [a]
Balsam $\overline{X}$ 48			—	19 [a]
Henna $\overline{X}$ 29				—

Nemenyi's test for pairwise comparisons following Friedman test.
Mean differences in rank shown in table.
Critical difference = 10.2.

[a] $P < .05$.

Panthenol's strength relates primarily to its appeal to youth and to consumers with long hairstyles.

Respondents positively interested in panthenol use are considerably younger than those who do not consider using the ingredient; 47% of the former group versus 20% of the latter group is under 25. See Table 3.

Potential panthenol users often have long hair styles (44%) versus only 15% among those not considering panthenol. Additionally, a large proportion of respondents describe Silky with panthenol as a product to be used with long hair (48%). See Table 4.

SUMMARY

Product performance research determines whether consumers will repurchase a brand after actually using it. This type of research measures after-use product ratings, both on an overall basis and with regard to specific product characteristics.

Product performance research may be conducted when the product is in the early stages of formulation. Various formulations are tested until one or more meet marketing's performance standards.

In some cases, an existing brand may be considered for reformulation. The reasons for doing reformulations include such factors as controlling production costs or turning around poor sales trends. A replacement product is recommended for marketplace introduction when product placement research indicates it performs superior to the existing product formulation.

Product performance research also is conducted for new product entries. Brand management may request the development of a specific formulation that can deliver specific benefits to be used as advertising claims. This product is

TABLE 3.   Age among Those Positively and Not Positively Interested in Buying "Silky" Hair Conditioner with Panthenol

Age	Positive (60–100 Purchase Intent) (%)	Negative (Less than 60 Purchase Intent) (%)
Under 25	47	20
25–34	28	39
35–49	16	32
50 and over	9	9
Median age	26	32
Total	100	100
Base	(70)	(50)

TABLE 4.   Description of Hair among Those Positively or Not Positively Interested in Buying "Silky" Hair Conditioner with Panthenol

Hair Descriptions	Positive (60–100 Purchase Intent) (%)	Negative (Less than 60 Purchase Intent) (%)
Specific hairstyles (net)	83	83
Have bangs	22	41
A shag	22	19
Wear my hair up	8	22
Wear it parted down the middle	17	9
Swept back from face	8	11
Wear it parted down the side	7	8
All other specific hairstyle mentions	24	23
Length of hair (net)	67	63
Long	44	15
Short	11	24
Normal or medium length	6	13
Shoulder length	6	11
Color of hair (net)	22	15
Blond	6	6
Frosted	—	6
All other color of hair mentions	15	4
Miscellaneous (net)	52	33
Casual look or free and long	14	6
Wear a beret or ribbons in my hair	6	4
Tease my hair	6	2
All other miscellaneous mentions	3	6
Total [a]		
Base	(70)	(50)

[a] Totals to more than 100% because of multiple mentions.

then tested to make sure it performs in line with its claims—and does not have unexpected weaknesses.

Sometimes, product performance research determines how a product actually performs among consumers who show interest in the product's concept. In this case, concept and product performance may be measured as one variable to project sales levels. By simulating market conditions, product performance research is used to estimate a brand's success.

TECHNICAL APPENDIX

ALTERNATE DESIGNS FOR PRODUCT PERFORMANCE RESEARCH

Design Alternatives	Notes
Unit of analysis Category user Category purchaser Company brand user Company brand purchaser	Generally, category users are sampled. When a product is being repositioned or a line extension is under consideration, company brand users are involved as well
Data collection method Personal Telephone Mail	Personal placement is most frequent. Placements are also made by mail. Data collection after use may be by any method; telephone is popular because of its economy and swiftness
Stimulus presentation Brand unidentified Brand identified	Blind placements (that is, brand is unidentified) are typical to remove the name influence
Consumer response Monadic Repeat	Single measures are costly, requiring larger samples for necessary sensitivity. They are purer tests, uninfluenced by the placement or trial of sets of products. Side-by-side repeat measures may not provide sufficient product experience for a valid response
Evaluation criteria Competitor brand(s) Company brand	A new product will use a competitive standard. When a product change is at stake, the company's current product becomes the basic yardstick

ANALYTICAL TECHNIQUES

This section covers selected ANOVA techniques for analyzing product performance and other studies. Emphasis here is given to studies that use single, score level measurement and two or more independent variables.* A nonparametric test on repeat-ranked observations is presented.

*If the reader's immediate interest is in designs with several independent variables, repeat measure ANOVA designs, turn to the Technical Appendix of the next chapter.

Specific techniques treated in this section are completely randomized factorial two- and three-way ANOVAs, split-plot, between-between-within ANOVA, and the Friedman test. The extensions of simpler, single measure analyses of variance introduce complexities of analysis that require careful attention.

Completely Randomized Factorial Two-Way ANOVA

The completely randomized factorial two-way ANOVA tests the effects of each of two independent variables and their interaction on a dependent variable. The assignment of respondents to completely crossed treatment combinations is randomized, and each respondent appears in one and only one design cell.

For example, a shoe manufacturer may be interested in measuring satisfaction with four shoe models: high-heeled brown, high-heeled black, low-heeled brown, low-heeled black. Prospects would be "placed" with only one of these models on a random assignment basis. After use for a specified period, satisfaction ratings would be taken. A key test would be for the interaction— that is, significant differences between individual models—described by the two variables of color and heel height.

The reasons this technique would be chosen over a completely randomized design include the following:

More information is given: main effects, as well as interactions.
Greater efficiency: more sensitivity for the sample size.
Greater stability of results: larger samples for main effects.

Analysis 6.1. "Vita Punch" Soft Drink

In Case 6.1, Vita Punch, a substitute ingredient was tested. A two-way analysis of variance (formulation and sex were the independent variables) showed no difference in performance for formulations. The substitute ingredient outperformed the current ingredient among women when a significant interaction was analyzed.

Completely Randomized Factorial Three-Way ANOVA

Three independent variables and four interaction effects on a dependent variable are involved in the completely randomized factorial three-way ANOVA. In the shoe manufacturer example, a third variable, buckled versus laced, might be introduced into the study. In this case, respondents would be assigned randomly to one of eight cells: high-heeled brown buckled, high-heeled black buckled, high-heeled brown laced, high-heeled black laced, low-heeled brown buckled, low-heeled black buckled, low-heeled brown laced, low-heeled black laced. A key test would be for the "second order interaction," meaning the significance of differences between all eight specific models.

The completely randomized factorial three-way ANOVA is very useful and efficient for some kinds of research problems. In other cases, the technique should be avoided, since practical problems in controlling the study may arise and the interpretation of interactions may be needlessly complex.

Analysis 6.2. "Perma-Mist" Hair Spray

In Case 6.2, Perma-Mist, a three-way, completely randomized factorial ANOVA was used to reach a decision about a valve design for the spray. Two other independent variables were included in the analysis to control results for biases due to consumer characteristics. The Wide Valve design outperformed the Narrow Valve on the main effect. The interaction tests were generally supportive of the conclusion; that is, no results ran counter to the overall conclusion.

Split-Plot, Between-Between-Within ANOVA

The split-plot, between-between-within ANOVA calls for repeat measures on one independent variable and for single measures on each of two other independent variables. For example, a carpet manufacturer might be interested in the potential popularity of five carpet patterns for several carpet sizes and materials (e.g., wool vs. nylon). Each prospect in a test would be shown all five designs but would see only one size and one material (presumably, the size and material of greatest interest to a given respondent). The results of the analysis would tell whether the second order interactions—patterns within size and material—are significantly different in potential popularity.

Use of this design is indicated when two of the independent variables represent givens that respondents bring to a test situation; the third variable is the unknown response to the test material in combination with the first two independent variables.

Analysis 6.3. "Carry Kleen" Hand Cleanser

In Case 6.3, Carry Kleen, each respondent received two products to use (order of use was randomized). Respondents' occupational class and their regular product were used to stratify responses to the two products. A split-plot, between-between-within analysis showed no significant difference in performance between the two products. Analysis of significant interactions showed that occupational segments exist for each product.

The Friedman Test

When data are analyzed on a rank level of measurement and the ranks are for the same individuals throughout several conditions, the Friedman test is appropriate. For example, a test of three jogging suit materials might be designed so that each of the three is worn (randomly sequenced) by every respondent. To indicate preference, rank orders of 1, 2, 3 are assigned to each model for every respondent. The results of a Friedman test would indicate whether differences between jogging suits are significant.

The Friedman test is conservative in that it assumes neither normality nor homogeneity of variances. It does make one assumption that should be considered seriously—there are no ties in ranks.

Analysis 6.4. "Silky" Hair Conditioner

In Case 6.4, Silky, respondents were exposed to all four potential ingredients, randomly presented. The Friedman test was used to analyze differences in response to the four names. The analysis disclosed significant differences in the potentials of the ingredients to strengthen the basic product concept.

COMPUTER ANALYSIS

A numerical example of the completely randomized factorial ANOVA is presented in this section. The purpose of this analysis is to test for the interaction effect of several independent variables.

TABLE 6.2. Completely Randomized Factorial Anova

COMPLETELY RANDOMIZED FACTORIAL ANOVA (SAS BATCH)

ANALYSIS

DEPENDENT VARIABLE: RESPONSE

SOURCE	DF	SUM OF SQUARES
MODEL	7	180.96875000
ERROR	24	18.75000000
CORRECTED TOTAL	31	199.71875000
SOURCE	DF	ANOVA SS
A*B	7	180.96875000

Analysis Plan: Completely Randomized Factorial ANOVA

Each of 32 respondents is measured once and for one treatment combination (i.e., one level of each independent level, crossed into a single treatment). As shown in Table 6.1, there are two independent nominal variables: A, with two levels; and B, with four levels.

TABLE 6.1. Completely Randomized Factorial Anova

COMPLETELY RANDOMIZED FACTORIAL ANOVA (SAS BATCH)

ANALYSIS OF VARIANCE PROCEDURE

CLASS LEVEL INFORMATION

CLASS	LEVELS	VALUES
A	2	1 2
B	4	1 2 3 4

NUMBER OF OBSERVATIONS IN DATA SET = 32

VARIANCE PROCEDURE

MEAN SQUARE	F VALUE	PR > F	R-SQUARE	C.V.
25.85267857	33.09	0.0001	0.906118	15.8013
0.78125000		STD DEV		RESPONSE MEAN
		0.88388348		5.59375000

VALUE	PR > F
33.09	0.0001

Interpretation

The analysis of Table 6.2 (pages 126 and 127) tests significance of the differences in the treatment means for the interactions of the two levels of variable B with four levels of variable A. The significance level is shown as 0.0001 ($F = 33.09$, df $= 7$). The effect of combinations of treatment variables on RESPONSE is significant.

Computer Output

Table 6.2 shows the analysis of variance for the dependent variable, RESPONSE. In this example, the model shows F, df, and probability for the interaction of the two independent variables (i.e., of their joint effects on RESPONSE). The df for the model has pooled df for A and B interaction and df for the main effects A and B. The error term used to test significance is the residual variance, when variance due to the first order interaction and the main effect has been removed.

SEVEN

Packaging Impact

Management knows that the details of packaging may affect its brand's consumer acceptance. Therefore, you, the researcher, are asked to design studies that measure the impact of packaging on consumers' purchase interest.

"Packaging impact" refers to how the brand's packaging affects consumers in terms of (1) identifying the brand, (2) attracting customers, and (3) creating brand preference. Good packaging impact results from immediate attraction, brand recognition, and visual recall.

In the preceding chapters, I branched out from marketing strategy problems to cover specific problems of the viability of product concepts and product performance. In this chapter, I continue with problems related to packaging and its impact on consumers. Further, I show how to design and analyze packaging impact studies.

Increase visual selling force of package designs. The research you do tells the kind of job a package will do as a personal sales representative for a brand. Package decisions, based on the work you do, result in consumer impressions of important differences between brands. These differences affect brand choices even when purchases are planned. The differences give the edge to a well-packaged brand. When package design is a strong visual selling force, there is an increase in impulse buying for the brand as well.

Find out if package communications are "on strategy" for a brand. Package communications may identify the product category, brand name, uses and users of the product, use occasions, product features, and brand image. Consumer research provides a means of learning whether these packaging communications can be coordinated with the brand's entire marketing program. You, the researcher, evaluate if a package's shape, picture, symbols, color, material, and dimensionality are a harmonious blend, representing a brand's personality.

You select packages with favorable impact by doing several kinds of studies, such as those in Exhibit 7.1.

Research problems in Exhibit 7.1 show special types of package impact assignments. These problems may be classified by (1) longer-term distribution

EXHIBIT 7.1.   Examples of Packaging Impact Problems

Research Problems	Scope of Package Design
Improving packages	Continuity of design
Selecting on-pack offers	Product promotion
Replacing packages	Total redesign
Finding packages for new products	New design or "family" identification

versus short-run promotions and (2) continuity or change of design for existing products versus new design or family identification for new products.

Now, let's turn to the first of these research problems.

IMPROVING PACKAGES

When the basic packaging design is adequate, a simple revision may lead to improvements. Packaging revision involves making changes, often subtle ones, that fine tune packaging.

The object of packaging revision is to reenlighten the consumer about the presence and character of a brand. The product manager wants the brand's packaging to enhance the existing brand image. She wants to spotlight her brand's best features by tightening up current packaging features. Packaging improvements may involve making changes in the shade of a particular color used or in the angles, locating sizes, and details of particular design elements. These changes represent an opportunity to freshen up the package and upgrade the brand's quality image.

Packaging revision research tests whether alternative executions of current packaging will improve the brand's appeal. Also, it provides a check on whether the result of a change will be to reinforce or strengthen the existing brand image.

A revised package may be recommended for marketplace use if it does a better job than the original of integrating package design elements. In such cases, research may show that consumers are more favorable to the revised packaging's aesthetics.

Case Preview: "Arise" Instant Breakfast Drink

Case 7.1, Arise, showed differences in purchase interest for four alternatives of the product's packaging; the packages were basically the same but differed in two respects: location of promotional copy (riser flap or no riser flap) and promotional copies (two versions).

The Promotions department conferred with Research and Marketing about this project and prepared the test packages. The results of the study showed a significant interaction between copy content and copy placement, and the riser flap promotional copy "Get up and go" was recommended for marketplace use.

Case 7.1   "Arise" Instant Breakfast Drink Flap Study

Objective

Arise Instant Breakfast Drink's current packaging has no riser flap; its package copy emphasizes the product's wake-up benefit. The objective of this study is to evaluate two different versions of copy on a riser flap, compared with the Arise basic package. They are as listed here:

Get up and go (flap and package).
Get up and go (package only).
Wake up (flap and package).
Wake up (package only).

Method

Each of four Arise packages (two with a riser flap, two without a riser flap) was exposed in one presentation to a single group of 50 female instant breakfast drink buyers. Interviewing was conducted in a high traffic shopping center.

The basic criterion measure for evaluating the copy and the flap was a 10-point, constant sum purchase allocation scale. Respondents were asked to divide 10 points between the four randomly arranged items they were shown to reflect how interested they were in purchasing each item, based on the way it was presented to them. A randomized block factorial ANOVA was used to determine if a single combination of copy and copy location promised to do the best job in the marketplace.

Recommendations and Conclusions

The riser flap copy "Get up and go" is recommended for marketplace use. "Get up and go" scores above the alternatives tested on the criterion 10-point purchase allocation measure. The average scores for the four Arise copy or flap alternatives are shown in Table 1.

The results of the randomized block factorial ANOVA show a significant interaction between copy content and copy placement. It is apparent that only the "Get up and go" flap and package average score (3.5) is significantly greater than the "Wake up" package only control score (2.0). From analysis of the main effects, it is seen that either copy or the location of the copy alone are not significant in the way they affect purchase allocation. See Table 2.

When asked what the riser copy alternative tells them about Arise, 97% of the prospective buyers exposed to the winning option mention some positive

TABLE 1.   Average Purchase Allocation for Two Copy Approaches Presented in Two Different Ways on Packaging for "Arise"

Copy Placement	Copy		Total
	Get Up and Go	Wake Up	
Flap and package	3.5(50) [a]	2.2(50)	5.7(100)
Package only	2.3(50)	2.0(50)	4.3(100)
Total	5.8(100)	4.2(100)	10.0(200)

[a] Numbers in parentheses indicate the total number of scores on which each average is based.

TABLE 2.   Sources of Variation in Purchase Allocation for Two Copy Approaches Shown in Two Different Ways on Packaging for "Arise"

Sources of Variation	MS=Mean Square	F	df	Significance Level
Copy	1.17	.89	1	N.S. $(P > .05)$
Copy placement	.83	.66	1	N.S. $(P > .05)$
Respondents	—	—	49	(Not computed)
Copy × Copy placement	51.62	27.21	1	$P < .05$
Copy × Respondents	2.41		49	
Copy placement × Respondents	2.66		49	
Copy × Copy placement × Respondents	2.17		49	
Total			199	

aspect of the product. Relatively few (13%) mention some negative aspect of the product, as shown next:

Aspect of Product	Net of Positive Mentions (%)	Net of Negative Mentions (%)	Difference Positive− Negative (%)
Get up and go flap and package	97	13	84
Get up and go package only	87	33	54
Wake up flap and package	89	26	63
Wake up package only	93	20	73
Base	(50)	(50)	(50)

Specific interpretations of what the package and flap copy "Get up and go" means provides insights into the strengths of the winning entry. Comments about this copy relate to the energizing aspect of the product—for example, that the product "gives you energy" (40%).

A possible explanation of the results for the "Get up and go" package and flap alternative is that the phrase, when placed immediately after the name Arise (on the flap), strengthens the energizing image of the product. See Table 3.

TABLE 3.   What Copy or Riser Flap Tells about "Arise" Product

Response	Get Up and Go Flap and Package (%)	Get Up and Go Package Only (%)	Wake Up Flap and Package (%)	Wake Up Package Only (%)
Positive mentions				
(net)	99	87	89	93
Gives energy	40	33	29	27
Helps you wake up	27	27	25	20
Good tasting	27	—	12	17
Low in calories	13	20	14	7
Easy to prepare	10	13	9	10
Has vitamins	7	10	11	17
Negative mentions				
(net)	13	33	26	20
Don't understand what copy means	10	20	15	7
Means nothing to me	—	7	4	3
Can't believe what it says	—	3	5	3
Same as other instant breakfast drinks	3	3	2	4
Total[a]				
Base	(50)	(50)	(50)	(50)

Question: (Point to statements on package or flap) What does this statement (read statement) tell you about this product? Anything else?

[a]Total exceeds 100% because of multiple mentions.

SELECTING ON-PACK OFFERS

Sometimes packaging is revised for a limited time period and a special purpose. Use of on-pack consumer promotions for a brand is an important marketing tool. These promotions serve as an added incentive for consumers to purchase the brand. Examples of on-pack promotions are premium merchandise (with the proof of purchase on or inside the packaging), price discounts, and extra product quantities with purchase.

Promotional packaging research isolates the particular promotion with the greatest potential for attracting sales that might otherwise have been lost. The complete evaluation of on-pack promotion takes into account the value of the customer attracted by the promotion. Attraction of new or past users who show a strong possibility of becoming frequent and regular purchasers of the brand indicates greater value for a promotion, other things considered.

The strongest promotions will increase first-time trial and tempt former users into returning for another purchase. The promotion finally chosen for use with the brand takes into account the net improvement estimated in brand sales and the cost and liabilities associated with the promotion.

Promotional packaging research is expected to have a greater payoff in a market in which brands are less differentiated. Before a product manager approves use of a promotion for a brand, research will provide assurance that the promotion will project the brand's image favorably.

Case Preview: "Hilight" Shampoo and Conditioner

In Case 7.2, Hilight, research provided marketing with an indication of vitality for a promotion that was considered. The brand was quickly losing market share, and the promotion was suggested. An offer for a horseshoe charm and chain was imprinted on the package, together with a mail-in coupon. Research recommended a design for measuring the effect of the offer, and the combination of offer, competitive choice, and product type on purchase disposition.

The marketing and promotions departments approved this design. The product manager worked out the details on the costs of the charm and chain and the expected payoffs. The research indicated that the horseshoe charm and chain was a good promotion: the offer significantly affected purchase allocation.

Case 7.2   Evaluation of an On-Pack Promotion for "Hilight" Shampoo and Conditioner

Objective

A premium promotion for Hilight Shampoo is under consideration by marketing. The premium is a horseshoe charm and chain. The purpose of this research is to find out if the horseshoe offer shows enough vitality to warrant further consideration.

The offer for a horseshoe charm and chain for $2 is imprinted on all packages of Hilight Shampoo. A mail-in coupon appears on the back of the offer card. The copy on the card reads: "Good Luck Horseshoe Necklace Offer. $10.00 value for only $2.00 with this purchase. Lucky horseshoe believed to prevent illness, help win or keep the affection of the one you love."

Method

The objective of this study was met by conducting interviews with women, aged 18–49, who reported using shampoos and conditioners. Respondents were recruited in a shopping center. A group of 50 women (balanced for brands used) were used. Each member of the group was shown eight different pictures in randomized order. The pictures contained two products—a Hilight shampoo or conditioner or a brand Y shampoo or conditioner. Each picture contained only one type of product. Half of the pictures showed Hilight with the horseshoe charm and chain offer, and half did not make this offer.

For each picture shown, respondents were asked to express a preference on a constant sum measure, indicating their interest in purchasing Hilight or the competitive product. This constant sum measure was the primary criterion for evaluating the results of the test.

A three-way within ANOVA was used to test the effects of the offer and combinations of the offer, competitive choice, and product type on purchase predisposition.

Recommendations and Conclusions

The horseshoe charm and chain offer warrants further consideration for use as a promotional item for Hilight's shampoo and conditioner products.

These products, bearing the horseshoe offer, outscore the same products without the offer. Each is compared, on a paired basis with common controls, brand X and brand Y. The average rating for Hilight with the horseshoe offer is 4.9; the average rating without the offer is 4.2.

The results of a randomized block factorial ANOVA show that the offer significantly affects purchase allocation. In addition, this analysis indicates that the offer truly is effective with Hilight shampoo. Brand X is expected to experience significant losses when Hilight's shampoo with the offer competes with brand X's shampoo. See Tables 1 and 2.

The value of the horseshoe offer is generally good: four of five respondents indicate that it is worth $2. See Table 3.

Aesthetically, however, the horseshoe offer may be improved further. The horseshoe has low aesthetic rating; only about two of five respondents (17%) find it "very attractive." Fewer still say they would give it as a gift (13%). See Tables 4 and 5.

REPLACING PACKAGES

In some cases, a brand's basic packaging design is suspect. A product manager then will consider a distinctively new packaging design to replace the brand's current packaging. One aim of repackaging may be to revitalize the brand by changing its brand image in a more-acceptable direction. Another objective

TABLE 1. Average Purchase Allocation for the On-Pack Promotion for "Hilight" Compared to a Nonpromotional Presentation for "Hilight" (for "Hilight" Shampoo and Conditioner versus Corresponding Products for Brand X and Brand Y Competitors)

Product	"Hilight" with Offer	"Hilight" with No Offer	Average
Shampoo			
Competitor			
Brand X	5.6 (50)[a]	4.4 (50)	5.0 (100)
Brand Y	4.5 (50)	3.9 (50)	4.2 (100)
Conditioner			
Competitor			
Brand X	5.2 (50)	4.4 (50)	4.8 (100)
Brand Y	4.3 (50)	4.1 (50)	4.2 (100)
Average	4.9 (200)	4.2 (200)	4.6 (400)

[a]Numbers in parentheses indicate the total number of scores on which each average is based.

TABLE 2. Sources of Variation in Purchase Allocation for the On-Pack Promotion for "Hilight" Compared to a Nonpromotional Presentation for the Brand

Sources of Variation	MS = Mean Square	F	df	Significance Level
Offer	18.84	7.22	1	$P < .05$
Product	11.91	2.83	1	N.S. $P > .05$
Competitor	6.91	1.79	1	N.S. $P > .05$
Respondents	Not computed		49	$P < .05$
Offer × Product	25.79	6.20	1	$P < .05$
Offer × Competitor	14.63	6.71	1	$P < .05$
Product × Competitor	11.51	2.21	1	$P < .05$
Offer × Respondents	2.61	—	49	
Product × Respondents	4.21	—	49	
Competitor × Respondents	3.86	—	49	
Offer × Product × Competitor	15.94	5.54	1	$P < .05$
Offer × Product × Respondents	4.16	—	49	
Offer × Competitor × Respondents	2.18	—	49	
Product × Competitor × Respondents	5.12	—	49	
Offer × Product × Competitor × Respondents	2.93	—	49	
Total			399	

TABLE 3. Perceived Value of Horseshoe Charm and Chain Offer

Issues of Concern	Response (%)
Is charm and chain worth $2?	
Yes	77
No	23
What do you think charm and chain are worth?	
$3.00	3
1.50	14
1.25	3
Don't know	3
Total	100
Base	(50)

Questions: Do you think the charm and chain, as shown in the offer, are worth $2? How much do you think the charm and chain are worth?

TABLE 4. Aesthetic Perception of Horseshoe Charm and Chain

Rating	Response (%)
Very attractive	17
Somewhat attractive	50
Not attractive	33
Total	100
Base	(50)

Question: Would you say that the charm and chain is very attractive, somewhat attractive, not attractive?

TABLE 5. Perception of Horseshoe Charm and Chain as a Gift Item

Responses to Charm and Chain as a Gift Item	Respondents (%)
Yes	13
No	87
Total	100
Base	(50)

Question: Would you be interested in giving the charm and chain as a gift to someone?

may be to improve profitability by a changeover to more economical packaging.

Research criteria for recommending new packaging include whether the packaging conveys the new character of the brand called for in the marketing plan. The research must confirm the value of the strategy for repackaging to go ahead.

Repackaging may be coordinated with other efforts to revitalize a brand—product improvements, new advertising strategy, and so on. A product improvement may be indicated by copy on the changed packaging; redesigned package graphics may suggest the character of a product change. A new advertising slogan or logos may appear on the replacement packaging.

The introduction of a new package design can make a large contribution cumulatively. This is because packaging changes are infrequent; a package keeps working for a brand for an extended time period.

Case Preview: "Aspatrex" Aspirin

Case 7.3, Aspatrex, was a study in which a new package for a product was tested against the current packaging. This company wanted to introduce a more contemporary package for Aspatrex (in several sizes) and considered using either black lettering (current) or blue lettering. This research was commissioned to measure the relative impact of each of these colors on either the new or current packaging for several sizes of Aspatrex. The packaging experts who designed the new packaging thought it would be more effective. The involved parties awaited results from this packaging impact study. This study, surprisingly for the experts, indicated that the new packaging did not meet the criterion of outperforming the current packaging, and it was not considered further. Another important research finding was that the large package with the black lettering had higher preference scores than the large package with blue lettering. It was inferred that black lettering might be important to the success of large size Aspatrex.

Case 7.3   Test of a New Package for "Aspatrex" Aspirin

Objective

A new package has been designed for Aspatrex tablets. The new package is designed to convey a more contemporary look than the present package. This research is intended to evaluate the newly designed package and the relative impact of black lettering compared to blue lettering on either new or current packaging for Aspatrex.

Method

A personal, in-home survey was conducted to evaluate the new Aspatrex package among users of aspirin. The respondents were shown four packages randomly of new and current Aspatrex, each in a small and large size. To show their degree of purchase interest, respondents were asked to allocate 10 points between the four Aspatrex items. The design was replicated among independent samples of 60 respondents: one sample saw only packaging with black lettering; the other saw only packaging with blue lettering.

A 10-point purchase allocation measure was the criterion variable. For the new package design to be recommended as a replacement for the package now used, the new package had to score at least as high overall as the current package and higher than the current package in either the large or small size.

Recommendations and Conclusions

The new packaging design for Aspatrex is rejected from further consideration. It completely fails to meet the criterion of outperforming current packaging on at least one size and of being at least equal to the current packaging on an overall basis.

A split-plot, between-between-within ANOVA shows that current packaging significantly outperforms the new packaging on purchase allocation. There is a significant preference for larger sizes—a fact supported by the history of greater unit sales for the large size. Preference for the large size significantly improves for black lettering, the lettering used on current packaging. This suggests that the black lettering is a force for inducing customers to trade up to larger sizes and that use of this lettering should be continued. For overall consumer sales, however, the ANOVA suggests that letter color will make no difference. See Tables 1 and 2.

Package impressions of Aspatrex with the new design score lower than Aspatrex with the current design as "a package that tells me all I need to know."

For the small-size package, new design scores significantly lower than current on being informative; there is no real difference in this regard between current and new designs for the large size. See Table 3.

Regardless of package size, the current Aspatrex design is stronger than the

TABLE 1.   Average Purchase Allocation for Current and New "Aspatrex" Package Designs in Small and Large Sizes Presented with One or Two Colors for Letters

| Type of Lettering | Small Size | | Large Size | |
	New Design	Current Design	New Design	Current Design
Blue	1.9(60) [a]	2.6(60)	2.6(60)	2.8(60)
Black	2.0(60)	2.3(60)	2.5(60)	3.2(60)
Average	1.9(120)	2.5(120)	2.6(120)	3.0(120)

[a] Numbers in parentheses indicate the total number of scores on which each average is based.

TABLE 2. Sources of Variation in Purchase Allocation for Current and New "Aspatrex" Designs in Small and Large Sizes and One of Two Letter Colors

Sources of Variation	MS = Mean Square	F	df	Significance Level
Between respondents	—	—	119	
Letter color	1.90	.93	1	N.S. $P > .05$
Error: between respondents	2.40		118	
Within respondents			360	
Size	24.96	12.67	1	$P < .05$
Design	17.32	8.79	1	$P < .05$
Letter color × Size	12.57	6.38	1	$P < .05$
Letter color × Design	4.37	2.51	1	N.S. $P > .05$
Size × Design	7.33	3.03	1	N.S. $P > .05$
Letter color × Size × Design	7.91	3.27	1	N.S. $P > .05$
Error: within respondents			354	
Error₁: within respondents	1.97		118	
Error₂: within respondents	1.74		118	
Error₃: within respondents	2.42			
Total			479	

new one in suggesting effectiveness in relieving pain. The advantage of the current design in suggesting pain relief is greater for the smaller size.

A higher proportion of respondents regard the current design effective because "the label says 'relieves pain.' " Also, respondents are more likely to indicate "label states fast relief" for the current design than for the new design. The new design, however, is more likely than the current design to receive mentions of "relieves headache" as a reason for the package suggesting effectiveness in relieving pain. See Tables 4 and 5.

FINDING PACKAGES FOR NEW PRODUCTS

The impact of packaging changes for existing products has been discussed. But when a new product is involved, packaging impact is likely to be its greatest. The product manager sees the opportunity for new product packaging to

TABLE 3.   A Package That Tells Me All I Need to Know

Reaction	Small Size		Large Size	
	New Design (%)	Current Design (%)	New Design (%)	Current Design (%)
Definitely applies	23	41	47	47
	52	79	79	77
Probably applies	29	38	32	30
Might or might not	13	13	9	11
Probably does not apply	13	5	8	7
Definitely does not apply	21	3	3	4
Don't know or no answer	1	—	1	1
Total	100	100	100	100
Base	(120)	(120)	(120)	(120)

Question: I'm going to read a series of statements that may or may not describe this product. I would like you to tell me if you feel that the statement: "A package that tells me all I need to know . . ."

TABLE 4.   Rating of Package for Suggesting Effectiveness in Relieving Pain

	Small Size		Large Size	
	New Design (%)	Current Design (%)	New Design (%)	Current Design (%)
Effective in relieving pain	50	71	57	64
Not effective in relieving pain	50	29	43	36
Total	100	100	100	100
Base	(120)	(120)	(120)	(120)

Question: Is there anything about the package that suggests that the product is very effective in relieving pain?

communicate that the brand is a new entry, different and important to potential consumers. New packaging is closely linked to the concept for the new product.

The packaging selected through the research you do must perform well relative to expected competition. In the design of the research, the results of previous concept studies are examined for constructing a frame of competitive packages to be exposed to consumers. For new products there is a high level of uncertainty about the best packaging directions. Therefore, new product

TABLE 5.　Reasons for Rating Package as Suggesting Effectiveness in Relieving Pain

Reason	Small Size		Large Size	
	New Design (%)	Current Design (%)	New Design (%)	Current Design (%)
Not effective in relieving pain	50	29	43	36
Effective in relieving pain	50	71	57	64
Effective perceptions				
Says relieves pain	14	28	19	29
States fast relief	1	22	—	20
Says relieves headache	18	6	26	5
Ingredients shown	13	5	4	3
States relaxes you	—	—	2	3
Money back guarantee	—	5	1	8
Don't believe labels	—	—	1	—
Other	7	21	12	13
Don't know or no answer	—	1	1	1
Total	100	100	100	100
Base	(120)	(120)	(120)	(120)

Question: Is there anything about the package that suggests that the product is very effective in relieving pain? What would that be?

packaging research will often include more test variations than will other types of packaging impact studies.

The initial selection of packaging alternatives depends on the product manager's examination of competitors' packages—their package weaknesses and communications voids. The research evaluates the relative merits of test packaging in exploiting these opportunities to attract customers in the fierce competition on the shelf.

Case Preview:　"Detectaplac" In-Home Dental Plaque Test

In case 7.4, Detectaplac, research attempted to determine the effect of packaging on purchase interest for a brand, especially among weak, underdeveloped market segments. Detectaplac had shown a weakness in the 50 and over market. The researcher designed a study to find out, among different age segments, if Detectaplac did have packaging problems and how serious the problems might be.

The product manager was considering package revisions. Before investing time and money, she wanted to know if there really were packaging problems with this brand. The research showed that for each of the age segments there was no serious packaging-related weakness for Detectaplac.

Case 7.4 "Detectaplac" In-Home Dental Plaque Test Packaging Research

Objective

The objective of this research is to measure reaction to the Detectaplac package (vis-à-vis Brand X) within three age segments. Previous research has shown a weakness in Detectaplac's penetration in the 50 and older market. The present research specifically probes whether the packaging is a contributing factor to the brand's sub-par performance in this group.

Method

Qualified respondents were purchasers of in-home plaque tests. Personal interviews were completed with 120 qualified respondents. The 120 respondents were subdivided into three equal age group cells of 40 respondents each. Cells were defined as 18–34, 35–49, and 50 and over.

Respondents were first asked to divide 10 points between Detectaplac and brand X to express their degree of buying interest between the two brands. Afterward, respondents were shown two packages—one for each of the same brands. Once again, they were asked to indicate their buying preference among the two in-home plaque tests by dividing 10 points among the products.

The relative point allocation (in each age segment) for Detectaplac after exposure to the packages was to be the primary evaluation measure. The analysis called for a completely randomized design analysis of covariance (ANCOVA) that used the preexposure brand allocation as a covariate.

Recommendations and Conclusions

It is seen that for each age segment examined there is no serious packaging-related weakness for Detectaplac. After exposure to Detectaplac's packaging and that of brand X, the respondents generally reacted the same to the Detectaplac brand and brand X, regardless of the age group analyzed. The randomized design ANCOVA indicates that there is no statistically significant difference in packaging impact between the three age groups. See Tables 1 and 2.

Qualitatively, there is very consistent negative commentary about the Detectaplac brand. The ratings for brand impressions for Detectaplac are generally comparable to corresponding ratings for brand X on "value for money," "accuracy of results," and "ease of use." Detectaplac's one area of possible concern appears to be "confidence in the brand." See Table 3.

TABLE 1.   Average Purchase Allocation (10-Point Allocation) for "Detectaplac": Before Package Exposure, and after Package Exposure — Unadjusted and Adjusted (by Age)

Age	Average Purchase Allocation (10 Points)			
	Before Package Exposure	After Package Exposure	Adjusted after Package Exposure [a]	Base
18–34	5.64	5.31	5.03	(40)
35–49	5.43	5.24	5.09	(40)
50 and over	4.45	4.63	4.98	(40)

[a] After package exposure purchase allocation adjusted for variation in before package exposure purchase allocation

TABLE 2.   Sources of Variation in Purchase Allocation for "Detectaplac" for Three Age Groups

Sources of Variation	Adjusted MS=Mean Square	F	df	Significance Level
Age	2.86	.21	2	N.S. $P > .05$
Error	13.63			
Total			148	

TABLE 3.   Brand Impressions of Two In-Home Plaque Detection Products

Qualities Rated	Detectaplac	Brand X
Ease of use	7.5	7.7
Value for the money	7.0	6.8
Accuracy of results	6.8	6.7
Confidence in brand	6.4	6.9
Base	(120)	(120)

Question: Now, I'm going to ask you for your impression of the two brands on a scale ranging from 10, meaning excellent, to 1, meaning poor. How would you rate each of these brands on the following: accuracy of results; ease of use; confidence in brand; value for the money?

The two major strengths of the Detectaplac package are (1) the instructions on the box and (2) reference to the product's easy visibility. The window, a point of difference between Detectaplac and its competition, can have additional strategic importance for the brand: it can be used to distinguish Detectaplac from its competitors in future communications efforts. See Table 4.

Most respondents do not report anything disliked about Detectaplac. See Table 5.

TABLE 4. Likes about Detectaplac Package

Responses	Total Respondents (%)
Product likes	88
Instruction on the box, directions, informative, explains each step, has diagram	46
References to easy product visibility, "can see what you're buying," "you can see the product"	38
Likes color blue	15
Says "easy to use"	8
Like the stand	8
Convenient to use at home	8
Looks professional, implied dentist's approval	8
Tells you consult dentist	4
Everything is listed	4
Has a window	4
Points out importance of using product	4
Compact — all in one	4
Solution there already	4
Complete	4
Looks different	4
You know right away if you have plaque	4
Likes nothing	12
Base	(120)

Question: We would like to have you look at these packages again, and tell us, if you will, what, if anything, do you particularly like about each one?

TABLE 5. Dislikes about "Detectaplac" Package

Responses	Total Respondents (%)
No product dislikes (net)	85
Product dislikes (net)	15
Cover dull	4
Box unattractive	4
Not enough detail	4
No information on whether it works or not	4
Looks complicated	4
Base	(120)

Question: We would like to have you look at these packages again and tell us, if you will, what, if anything, do you dislike about each one?

SUMMARY

Packaging impact research measures whether a given package enhances or detracts from purchase interest. This type of research also investigates whether a package helps identify a brand and attracts customers. Packaging research is analyzed for its effect on brand image and to determine whether this image is related to the entire marketing program.

There are various types of packaging impact studies. One type deals with the problem of revising a basic package design. Packaging revision research tests the effect of alternative executions of current packaging on the brand's appeal and image.

In some cases a package is revised for a limited time period. For example, a marketing strategy study for shampoos indicated that consumers in this product category are highly receptive to on-package promotions when making brand choices. As a result, several on-pack promotions were proposed for one brand's packaging. Research was conducted to determine which of the proposed on-package promotions seemed most viable.

Another type of package impact study centers around introducing entirely new packaging for an existing brand. Usually, brand management will recommend introducing new packaging when it wants to revise the brand's image. In this case, research will be used to determine if the new packaging communicates the desired image.

When introducing an entirely new brand, packaging research is especially critical. Packaging must communicate that the brand is a new entry and important to target customers. Packaging research for new brands always compares a brand's packaging to that of competitive brands. For established brands, you, the researcher, will probably want to compare new packaging with competitive packages. You will also compare new packaging to current packaging. Research designs for these several types of packaging studies will differ in terms of the number of packaging alternatives included.

TECHNICAL APPENDIX

ALTERNATE DESIGNS FOR PACKAGING IMPACT RESEARCH

Design Alternatives	Notes
Unit of analysis Category user Category purchaser Company brand user Company brand purchaser	Frequently, category purchasers are sampled. When a package for an on-market product is changed, brand purchasers are included. Users are sometimes involved if there is a functional packaging issue

Design Alternatives	Notes
Data collection method Personal Telephone Mail	Typically, personal
Stimulus presentation Brand unidentified Brand identified	Invariably brand identified.
Consumer response Monadic Repeat	Repeat measures used (test, plus standard). Each package alternative generally exposed to a separate respondent cell
Evaluation criteria Competitor brands Company brand	Strongest design for a package change involves both company brand and competitive brand as standards

ANALYTICAL TECHNIQUES

The present section deals with repeat measure applications for packaging impact and other studies. In addition, a technique is shown using score data as one independent variable in the analysis of variance.

Specific techniques I will cover are randomized block factorial $a \times b \times s$ and $a \times b \times c \times s$ ANOVAs, split-plot, between-within-within ANOVA, and completely randomized design analysis of covariance (ANCOVA). Multifactor techniques emphasizing repeated measures are even more complex than those with single measures and require considerable reflection before they are applied.

Randomized Block Factorial $a \times b \times s$

The randomized block factorial $a \times b \times s$ ANOVA is a within-group technique. All a b treatment combinations are administered to each respondent. For example, suppose a company wanted to test two alternative packages. The research design might involve paired comparisons against four different competitors. Each respondent would be asked to make comparisons for eight randomly presented pairs of packages. The results could then be analyzed by a randomized block $a \times b \times s$ ANOVA.

Interpretation and decision making may become a problem, if the experiment results in interaction effects. One solution is to transform the data (e.g., to a trigonometric function) before the analysis to suppress interactions.

The potential cost efficiencies of this design are substantial. The randomized block factorial is more sensitive to significant differences than the completely randomized factorial, when costs are held constant. Use of the technique should be considered when the technique's assumptions are reasonably met.

Analysis 7.1. "Arise" Instant Breakfast Drink

In Case 7.1, Arise, four packages were shown to each respondent. Each package was a specific combination of package design and package copy. The randomized block factorial analysis showed that the interaction of design and copy was significant. A clear and positive recommendation for one specific alternative was the result.

Randomized Block Factorial $a \times b \times c \times s$

The randomized block factorial $a \times b \times c \times s$ involves each respondent with every combination of three treatments. The analysis provides significance tests for three separate variables (main effects), three two-way interactions, and one triple interaction. Because there are so many interaction terms, the researcher will sometimes pool (i.e., combine) these terms using this combination for all tests.

It is wise to consider a pilot test, if it is suspected that the large number of exposures called for will bias the test. If it is found that respondents become careless in their responses or break off the interview, the study can be redesigned.

Despite its complexities and complications, the randomized block factorial $a \times b \times c \times s$ technique should be used when suitable for a problem. There are several advantages that make the technique very attractive, in addition to obvious cost efficiencies: (1) biases associated with the timing of exposures in between-group studies are controlled, (2) unknown experimental conditions are less variable, and (3) results are faster than for sequential studies.

Analysis 7.2. "Hilight" Shampoo and Conditioner

In Case 7.2, Hilight, the problem called for testing the effect of an on-pack promotion. The design used three independent variables—offer, competitive choice, and product type. The three-way ANOVA design was felt to be useful, since it made the study aim less obvious to respondents. The analysis not only showed the potential effectiveness of the promotion but also located specific competitors as a result of the promotion.

Split-Plot, Between-Within-Within ANOVA

The split-plot, between-within-within ANOVA calls for blocking (single measures) on only one of three independent variables.

The number of effects to analyze is large: 14 basic statistics in the sources of variation layout. When the second order interaction is significant, the analysis may go even further to include tests of comparisons within small subcells.

As an example of this technique, suppose a sporting goods manufacturer is interested in marketing a newly designed tennis racket. Research to test the new racket's potential acceptance might call for two (between) groups—men and women. Within each group, respondents would be given four tests: singles, new racket; singles, standard racket, doubles, new racket; doubles, standard racket. The order of tests would be randomized for each respondent. Detailed analyses would tell whether the ratings of the new racket differ between men and women for singles matches.

Analyses for split-plot, between-within-within ANOVA require more attention to input and computation than most tests of variance. An extra input source involves the number of levels—that is, subgroups for each independent variable.

Analysis 7.3. "Aspatrex" Aspirin

In Case 7.3, Aspatrex, a new packaging design was under consideration. The test made use of a split-plot, between-within-within design. The single measure (between) variable was lettering color. The other two repeat variables were new and current basic designs and package size. The result of the analysis was a recommendation against a packaging change. The analysis provided additional assurance that the results were genuine.

Completely Randomized Design Analysis of Covariance (ANCOVA)

ANCOVA requires that a supplementary measure be added to the completely randomized ANOVA. This supplementary measure is used to lower the experimental error test statistic and thus improve the accuracy and reliability of the basic analysis.

An example might be a packaging test involving three alternatives for a brand. It might be decided to include shelf position as a variable in the test. Assume a test between three groups; each sees one alternative for the brand on a competitive shelf. Shelf position for the test package is randomly rotated in each group and becomes a control variable that equalizes and adjusts scores for its effect.

In some cases, the adjustment of means for a third variable will not be significant. A test can be made to determine this. Even when the difference between adjusted and unadjusted means is significant, the adjustment may not affect the study's conclusions. In either case, the analysis provides additional assurance that the results are genuine.

TABLE 7.1. Randomized Block Factorial Anova

RANDOMIZED BLOCK FACTORIAL ANOVA - (SAS BATCH)

ANALYSIS OF VARIANCE PROCEDURE

CLASS LEVEL INFORMATION

CLASS	LEVELS	VALUES
A	2	1 2
B	4	1 2 3 4
BLOCK	4	1 2 3 4

NUMBER OF OBSERVATIONS IN DATA SET = 32

TABLE 7.2. Randomized Block Factorial Anova

RANDOMIZED BLOCK FACTORIAL ANOVA = (SAS BATCH)

ANALYSIS

DEPENDENT VARIABLE: RESPONSE

SOURCE	DF	SUM OF SQUARES
MODEL	10	188.81250000
ERROR	21	17.15625000
CORRECTED TOTAL	31	205.96875000
SOURCE	DF	ANOVA SS
BLOCK	3	0.59375000
A*B	7	188.21875000

Analysis 7.4. "Detectaplac" In-Home Dental Plaque Test

In Case 7.4, Detectaplac, packaging was tested for a new product. The test was designed to assess the response to the product among specified age groups. Age groups were the independent variable of a completely randomized ANOVA. The ANCOVA was superimposed on the design to control results for initial preferences. The results showed no special weakness in packaging impact for the age groups involved.

COMPUTER ANALYSIS

A numerical example of the randomized block factorial ANOVA is presented in this section. The purpose of this analysis is to test for the interaction effect of several dependent variables and the block variable effect.

Analysis Plan: Randomized Block Factorial ANOVA

Each of four respondents is measured eight times. The eight measures represent the combination of all four treatment levels of variable B and the two treatment levels of variable A. The four block levels shown in Table 7.2 correspond to the four respondents. The 32 observations shown in the table are the treatment combinations-by-respondents cell entries.

RIANCE PROCEDURE

MEAN SQUARE	F VALUE	PR > F	R-SQUARE	C.V.
18.88125000	23.11	0.0001	0.916705	16.3410
0.81696429		STD DEV		RESPONSE MEAN
		0.90386077		5.53125000

VALUE PR > F

0.24 0.8659
32.91 0.0001

Computer Output

Table 7.1 shows the analysis of variance for the dependent variable RE-SPONSE. In addition to the test for the significance of the interaction of variables A and B, the model analyzes the block (respondent) effect. The df for the model has pooled df for the block, other main effects, and the double and triple interactions of the independent variables. The error term is the remaining, unexplained variance.

Interpretation

The analysis of Table 7.2 tests the significance of the differences in A B interactions when these observations are blocked by a third variable. The probability level for the A B interaction is significant (PR = 0.0001 F = 32.91, df = 7). The effect of the blocking variable is not significant (PR = 0.8659, F = 0.24 df = 3).

PART FOUR
PROMOTION RESEARCH

EIGHT
Advertising Quality

Advertising quality affects the returns on a brand's advertising investment. The research you do shows which advertisements will produce favorable effects among consumers, leading to better returns.

Chapter 5 discussed studies that tell what a brand's customers need and expect. Such information provides direction for creative work in advertising. In this chapter, I show how research measures the results of creative work—the quality of broadcast or print advertising. "Advertising quality" refers to how well an advertisement promotes a brand's appeal. Advertising has done its job when customers are convinced that the brand in question best meets their needs.

The studies conducted by you, the researcher, often test several advertisements for a brand. These tests screen commercials and ads before they can be used in the marketplace. Thus they assure acceptable levels of advertising quality for a brand. Let's see what you, the researcher, do to rate and improve a brand's advertising quality.

Find out how advertising communications affect consumers. The research you do measures the quality of an advertisement to communicate its strategic message, its memorability, and its power to persuade consumers to buy the brand. You try to select advertisements that meet these criteria successfully.

The studies are expected to assure that advertising communications will strengthen the consumer franchise.

Assist in making decisions about advertising strategy and execution. With advertising quality research, management makes the following kinds of decisions:

Setting advertising strategy objectives—for example, sales messages to communicate.

Coordinating creative objectives—that is, how to execute the advertising through appropriate spokespersons and slogans.

Requiring consistency of advertising strategy and copy.

Selecting advertisements for use in advertising media.

155

Show ways to make customers know and want a brand. Management concentrates its efforts on increasing sales or share for a brand. Good advertising quality can be vital for these efforts. Good advertising will improve market position by (1) alerting consumers to a brand, (2) imparting specific information about a brand, and (3) motivating brand trial and repeat purchase.

To assist in making decisions about advertising strategies and executions, you are asked to measure advertising quality. Studies of advertising quality can be divided into several types, as shown in Exhibit 8.1.

Exhibit 8.1 shows how some problems may be classified. The dimensions used in classification are (1) claims strategy or execution and (2) the medium (if any) involved, for example, TV or print.

The first of these problems, evaluating advertising claims, is covered next.

EXHIBIT 8.1.   Examples of Advertising Quality Problems

Research Problems	Focus of Evaluation
Evaluating advertising claims	Claims strategy alternatives
Choosing ways to present advertising	Alternative executions of a claims strategy
Deciding whether to air commercials	TV claims strategy or execution alternatives
Selecting print advertisements	Print claims strategy or execution alternatives

EVALUATING ADVERTISING CLAIMS

An advertising claim is the main selling point to be used in advertising a brand. It is the special part of the advertising that makes the sale. The selection of the best claim leads to the creation of a brand personality that has high appeal to consumers.

The product manager wants to make use of advertising claims that harmonize with the target market strategy. For example, if young people are heavier users of a product category than others and the claim is a special product feature of interest to heavier users, then the claim has met an important selection criterion. The decision to use a particular claim is not expected to be revised hastily; as long as desired results are obtained, the claim generally will not be changed.

Advertising claims selection research evaluates alternative claims—intended as suggested reasons for consumers to buy the advertised product. The evaluation insures that the advertising claim will strengthen the brand by enhancing the basic product concept (see Chapter 5).

Research may recommend an advertising claim if it is credible, relevant, desirable, and different from the claims of competitors. The claim, however, should not overpromise, given a product's known performance qualities. In some cases, the use of a claim requires additional research support—surveys documenting consumer preference for the advertised brand.

The number of claims tested in the research will vary, depending on (1) the complexity of performance of the particular product, (2) the product's newness, (3) the claims of the competitive field, and (4) previous knowledge of consumer needs and wants.

Case Preview: "Rescue" Shoe Waterproofing Product

In Case 8.1, Rescue, Research evaluated the relative strength of three alternative copy claims. The advertising agency with the Rescue account created these three new advertising claims for this established product. The specific research objective was to determine which of these new claims created highest purchase preference relative to a competitive brand.

A free-lance researcher was hired for this project by the manufacturer, not the advertising agency. He worked closely with the advertising agency to understand the objectives of the creative strategies.

The research conclusions stated that there were significant differences in purchase preference scores for the three claims. The best-scoring claim was recommended for use in the brand's advertising.

Case 8.1   Selection of Advertising Claims for "Rescue" Shoe Waterproofing Product

Objective

The basic objective of the research is to evaluate the overall performance of three Rescue advertising claims.

Method

Personal interviews were conducted with 360 blue-collar workers, ages 18 and over, who had worn working shoes in the past month. Each respondent was exposed to one of three positions for brand X. All positions were shown in a full-page, four-color format, with identical illustrations and equal-length body copy. A two-way, chi-square was used to test the significance of the differences in brand preference associated with the tested advertising claims.

Recommendations and Conclusions

On the basis of a measure of purchase preference, the *long-lasting* Rescue advertising claim is superior to the *convenient* and *doesn't discolor* claims tested. *Long-lasting* received three-fifths of the preferences between Rescue and brand X. The other Rescue claims were inferior to brand X. A two-way, chi-square test found the differences between the three Rescue claims to be significant.

The Rescue positions differed greatly in their performances on preference, ranging from a high of 60% for *long-lasting* to 33% for *doesn't discolor*. See Table 1.

When respondents were asked to express likes about the *long-lasting* claim, the basic *long-lasting* claim was mentioned most frequently (35% net). About a quarter (23%) indicated "nothing" liked about the Rescue *long-lasting* claim. See Table 2.

TABLE 1.   Preference between "Rescue" and Brand X for Three Different "Rescue" Advertising Claims

Preference (n = 120)	Advertising Claims		
	Long Lasting (%)	Convenient (%)	Doesn't Discolor (%)
Rescue	60	44	33
Brand X	40	56	67

Chi-square = 17.38; $P < .01$

Question: Please imagine that you are purchasing a shoe waterproofing product. I would like you to show me the product you would be most interested in buying.

TABLE 2.   "Long Lasting" Likes

Qualities	Total (%)
Long lasting (net)	35
It's guaranteed to be long lasting	20
100% satisfaction with how long it lasts	12
Refund if it doesn't last	10
The ad, layout, copy (net)	10
The way it's applied	10
It's effective	8
Dries quickly	5
Convenient, easy to use	2
All other mentions	8
Nothing	23
Base	(120)

Nearly two-thirds (65%) stated that they disliked nothing about the claim of *long-lasting*. Expressed dislikes were at very low levels. See Table 3.

When asked in which way they felt Rescue was superior to brand X, respondents most frequently mentioned *long lastingness* (28% net) and satisfaction with Rescue (22.). See Table 4.

TABLE 3.   "Long Lasting" Dislikes

Qualities	Total (%)
Product satisfaction compared to others (net)	13
That it is better than all others	7
Comparing itself to other products or naming specific brands	7
Putting down other brands or knocking other products	7
The name Rescue (net)	10
The name implies that your shoes are in bad condition	7
The name is misleading	5
Don't like the name Rescue	2
The way it's applied	8
Doubt that shoe waterproofing lasts for week	7
You have to use it every day	5
Shoe waterproofing can't last for week or not possible	2
Nothing	65
Base	(120)

TABLE 4.   How "Rescue" Is Superior to Brand X for "Long Lasting"

Qualities	Total (%)
Long lasting (net)	28
It holds up well over time	18
Lasts a week or only use it once a week	7
It's longer lasting	7
Satisfaction (net)	22
Satisfaction	17
A product users like	7
Don't know or never tried the brand	18
Application or form	12
Nothing	27
Base	(120)

CHOOSING WAYS TO PRESENT ADVERTISING

An advertising execution is the way in which the advertising claim is presented. It refers to such things as the reputation and appearance of a person in the advertising, the number of words of copy, and the size and perspective of the product shown. The selection of the best execution makes a brand more salient and helps to persuade the consumer to buy the advertised product. That key words suggesting important benefits are used provides no assurance of the advertising quality being acceptable.

The product manager wants the advertising execution to reinforce advertising claims. For example, a convincing presenter, presented convincingly, will strengthen the impression of the brand name and make the advertising claim more relevant. In product fields in which brands are less differentiated in what they offer consumers, the impact of the execution becomes extremely important for advertising quality.

Advertising execution research evaluates different ways of delivering the same product message. The reason for the evaluation is to provide the best way of telling the product's story.

An advertising execution will be recommended by research if the presenter, situation, copy phraseology, and mood work together to clearly and persuasively communicate the intended sales message. Unfortunately, this does not happen all the time. Advertising executions can be extremely confusing. For example, an advertisement showing a woman wearing sunglasses and sipping a drink may lead consumers to wonder if sunglasses or an alcoholic beverage is being sold.

Advertising execution research becomes very important when a change in the advertising claim takes place. The research must screen out executions that suggest a brand offers benefits, with accompanying undesirable features—for example, improperly presenting a detergent as strong, implying that it's rough for the hands.

Case Preview: "Solo" Sugar Substitute

In Case 8.2, Solo, research was requested to determine which of two alternative copy lines with the same theme had greater impact. The Creative department had developed two versions for an advertising theme that emphasized "less calories than sugar with the same taste." The research was conducted to determine which of these two versions created stronger purchase interest.

The manufacturer of Solo did not have its own marketing research department. Therefore, the manufacturer's advertising agency commissioned the research. Agency researchers conferred with company marketing personnel over basic brand strategies. The company helped to specify what should be measured and how the information was to be interpreted.

The research concluded that the shorter copy line had greater impact in stimulating purchase interest. Both copy lines, however, did not successfully communicate one of the product attributes, and research recommended that the issue be explored further.

Case 8.2   "Solo" Sugar Substitute Copy Research

Objective

The purpose of this study was to determine the impact of two voice-over copy lines for an announcer for a Solo TV commercial. Both lines convey the themes of less calories than sugar with the same taste. The two copy lines, designated "shorter copy" and "longer copy" are these:

Shorter Copy.   "Solo. Less than half the calories of sugar, and tastes like the real thing. Solo, for regular use."

Longer Copy.   "Solo. Results you can't possibly get with sugar. Solo, less than half the calories of sugar, and tastes like the real thing—no bitter aftertaste."

Method

Each of the two copy lines was exposed to a separate group of women who used sugar substitutes. The shorter copy line was exposed to 149 women; the longer copy line was exposed to 127 women. The basic criterion for evaluating each copy line was the percentage preferring the Solo product to its retail cash equivalent, that is a product versus a cash offer. Results were tested by means of a two-way (2 × 2) chi-square.

Recommendations and Conclusions

The shorter copy line is recommended for use. It is superior to the longer copy line, based on the cash versus product criterion measure. The two-way, chi-square test found the difference between copy lines (50 vs. 41%) to be significant. See Table 1.

The superiority of the shorter copy is supported by its higher ratings for

TABLE 1.   Preference between "Solo" and Cash for Two Copy Lines

Response	Shorter Copy (%)	Longer Copy (%)
Preference	$(n = 149)$	$(n = 127)$
Solo	58	41
Cash	42	59

Chi-square = 6.83; $P < .05$

Question: Suppose you have the choice of either taking this product or ——— in cash. Which would you rather have—the product or the cash?

"right amount of calories," "less calories than other brands," and "tasted like real sugar." It should be noted that ratings for both copy lines were relatively low on "tastes like real sugar." This image area should be explored in future creative copy development. See Table 2.

TABLE 2. Ratings of "Solo" on Three Product Attributes (by Copy Line)

Attributes	Shorter Copy (mean)	Longer Copy (mean)
Giving you the right amount of calories	6.12	5.26
Giving less calories than other brands	5.71	4.63
Tastes like real sugar	4.29	4.12
Base	(149)	(127)

DECIDING WHETHER TO AIR COMMERCIALS

Commercial testing provides a basis for deciding whether to show a commercial on television. By obtaining preliminary responses of consumers, it is possible to discriminate between alternative commercials.

Commercial testing evaluates the potential of commercials to build preference for the advertised brand. When an ongoing advertising program is "working," there usually is little interest in testing commercials. Commercial testing is most important when there is uncertainty and abrupt change in the advertising. For example, tests are more likely when "wearout" of an advertising campaign is suspected. "Wearout" refers to the falloff of effectiveness of presentations of an advertising theme because of such factors as increasing inattention and changes in consumer values. These are the most likely conditions for commercial testing:

A new product is introduced.

An existing campaign is revised.

A new campaign is prepared.

Commercials may be tested in rough or finished form. Conservatively, rough commercial test results may be measured against standards for other rough commercials. A frequent practice, however, is to compare the results for rough commercials directly with those for finished commercials, assuming a reliability between the scores of both types.

Two basic methods of testing commercials involve (1) "forced" or (2) natural exposure. Forced exposure takes place under experimental conditions. It involves presenting a commercial by itself or within a program format to cooperating respondents. The natural exposure method allows the respondent to view any programming under typical conditions, without any awareness of being in a test situation.

Forced and natural exposure techniques each have special purposes. Forced exposure techniques are used more frequently to test communication and persuasion. The natural exposure approach is used primarily to measure brand and message recall. It should be recognized that (1) there is some overlap in what the two techniques can measure and (2) it is possible, and sometimes desirable, to use both techniques for testing a single commercial.

Testing commercials is very valuable when such testing prevents a boomerang effect, meaning the opposite of an intended effect. A series of commercial tests can lead to important generalizations about advertising a brand.

Case Preview: "Downy-Q" Quilt

Case 8.3, Downy-Q, is an example of a commercial test that was conducted when an advertising campaign for an established brand had run its course. This revised campaign, "Fighting the Cold," emphasized that Downy was an "extra warm quilt"; Previous research demonstrated this to be an important and "deliverable" product quality. The commercial test was requested to measure the commercial's ability to generate purchase interest.

The Marketing department recommended this revised advertising campaign and was now anxious to know how effectively this commercial performed. The commercial test concluded that "Fighting the cold" is a persuasive commercial. The test also demonstrated that the revised commercial had greater appeal to specific market segments.

Case 8.3 "Downy-Q" Quilt Commercial Test

Objective

Based on previous research indicating that many people want extra warmth in a quilt, Downy-Q's agency has developed a new commercial for Downy-Q, "Fighting the cold." Research has been conducted to determine the interest generated in purchasing Downy-Q as a result of the commercial.

Method

Brand choices for the same individuals were obtained before and after commercial viewing. Shifts were tested by McNemar's χ^2_c. The commercial was tested in 30-second, color-moving, storyboard form in a theater test. Invited viewers were shown programming with commercial inserts. Qualified respondents were women who had bought quilts in outlets carrying Downy-Q.

Recommendations and Conclusions

"Fighting the cold" appears to be a very persuasive commercial, particularly among employed, married women. It is recommended that this commercial be added to those run for Downy-Q during the colder seasons as a potential means of expanding the number of users of the brand and possibly to increase replacement purchases among present owners of Downy-Q.

The overall changes in brand choice were measured, based on responses before the commercial was shown and those obtained after the commercial was shown. McNemar's test showed that the changes were significant: the commercial appeared to increase choices for Downy-Q.

"Fighting the cold" scores a +15 prepost increment. This is above the norm for quilt commercials (+10). The test commercial had a higher prepost among married (+17) than unmarried (+12). The prepost measurement was particularly high (+18) among respondents who are employed. Among respondents who are not employed the prepost score was +13. See Tables 1 and 2.

TABLE 1. Shifts in Choice of "Downy-Q" Quilt (before and after Showing of Commercial)

Brand Choice after Commercial	Brand Choice before Commercial	
	Downy-Q (n = 23) (%)	Other Brand (n = 237) (%)
Downy-Q	78	19
Other brand	22	81

McNemar's test:
Chi-square = 31.04; $P < .01$

Question: We are going to give away a series of prizes. If you are selected as one of the winners, which of the following would you truly want to win?

TABLE 2. Prepost Increment in Choice of "Downy-Q"

Demographic Group	"Fighting the Cold"		Norm: All Quilt Commercials	
	Base	Score	Average	Range
Total audience	(260)	+15	+10	6–19
By marital status				
Married	(130)	+17		
Not married	(130)	+12		
By age				
Under 35	(130)	+14		
35 and over	(130)	+15		
By employment status				
Not employed	(180)	+13		
Employed	(170)	+18		

Question: We are going to give away a series of prizes. If you are selected as one of the winners, which of the following would you truly want to win? (Check list.)

Respondents were asked to select adjectives to describe the commercial shown. Specific adjectives on which "Fighting the cold" scored lower than norm relate to the entertainment aspects of the commercial, whereas on adjectives relating to the copy content of the commercial, "Fighting the cold" scores as well as the norm. See Table 3.

Respondents were given a list of possible attributes of a quilt and asked to indicate which attributes apply to Downy-Q (after seeing the commercial). The audience of "Fighting the cold" indicates primarily that Downy-Q is "extra warm," "light weight," or has "pretty designs." See Table 4.

TABLE 3. Adjective Checklist for "Downy-Q" Quilt Commercial

Adjectives	"Fighting the Cold" (%)	Norm: All Quilt Commercials (%)
Positive adjectives		
Appealing	18	24
Clever	11	40
Convincing	20	14
Effective	19	23
Entertaining	5	24
Fast moving	12	21
Genuine	7	4
Imaginative	7	21
Informative	24	18
Interesting	13	17
Original	7	20
Realistic	8	3
Unusual	3	8
Negative adjectives		
Amateurish	9	11
Dull	33	20
Bad taste	4	4
Repetitious	17	16
Silly	8	19
Slow	8	7
Unbelievable	3	5
Unclear	3	2
Unimportant	14	14
Uninteresting	32	19

Question: Which of these words do you feel come closest to describing the commercial you've just seen? (Check list.)

TABLE 4. Product Attribute Checklist for "Downy-Q"

Attributes	"Fighting the Cold" (%)
Extra warm	56
Light weight	48
Pretty designs	45
Durable fabrics	28
Nice fabrics	27
Good construction	27

Question: Which of the following statements do you feel apply to Downy-Q? (Mark as many or as few as you feel apply.)

SELECTING PRINT ADVERTISING

Print ads that are effective get the reader's attention, deliver key messages, and make the advertised product appealing. They also perform best among preferred segments of consumers. Print ad testing aids in screening those ads in print form that will be most effective.

Natural exposure or experimental methods of exposure may be used in print ad testing. One natural exposure method is "split-run testing." With split-run testing, two or more ads are alternated in printed copies of an issue of a newspaper or magazine. Each ad usually contains an offer for the advertised product. The primary criterion of effectiveness in these tests is the difference between ads in the number of respondents requesting the product. When the difference is not decisive, information about responder characteristics may provide the necessary direction.

Recognition tests may be used under conditions of natural exposure to print ads. In these tests, respondents may be shown the actual magazine or paper and asked to indicate which ads they've read. The interpretation of an individual test is based on average scores for similar ads for the same brand. The interpretation of print ad recognition test results can be complicated. This is because the results reflect the advertising environment (number of pages in the magazine or newspaper, the location of the ad, and so on), physical features of the ad (its size and color composition), and the type of product advertised.

Experimental exposure methods are used more often to measure communications and buying attitude effects. A magazine may be given to respondents who are asked to read it. This magazine will contain a special "tipped-in" ad that was not printed in the actual issue. After a specific time (often 24—48 hours), respondents are reinterviewed and asked about their delayed recall of the advertising. Respondents are aided by being given a brand and product category cue. The results are scored for copy point registration and favorable attitude.

Other tests make use of immediate recall of print advertising exposed in the presence of an interviewer. Respondents may examine a stripped-down version of a magazine or a portfolio of ads. These tests probe specific factors affecting the performance of the ad: illustration, headline, and copy approach.

Case Preview: "Cocomoco" Cocoa Mix

Case 8.4, Cocomoco, was a print ad test that was conducted after split-run testing. The test involved two ads ("Real cocoa flavor" and "Take five"). Both ads were found to be equally effective. The Creative department wanted to know if both these commercials generated equal purchase interest. Another key question was which of the two ads did the best job to attract the brand's target market?

The researcher designed a study addressing the Creative department's question about target market response to the ads. The results indicated that one of the two ads, "Real cocoa flavor," did attract consumer segments against which the brand was targeted. Based on the split-run test and this follow-up study, Marketing selected "Real cocoa flavor" for the print ad campaign.

Case 8.4   "Cocomoco" Cocoa Mix Print Ad Selection Research

Objective

Two Cocomoco print ads were split-run tested in the *Kalamazoo Star*. As of the cutoff date, a total of 836 consumer product requests were received from both ads: 426 from the "Real Cocoa flavor" ad and 410 from the "Take five" ad. Based on experience, both ads seemed effective. The difference between ads in the number of requests for products was not decisive. Research was requested to help decide which of the two print ads would be more effective.

A telephone follow-up study among product requesters was conducted. The objective of the study was to find out whether the ads attract differing segments. The selection of the ad to use in a print campaign would be based on the similarity between responder profile and the strategic target market: primarily, adult women.

Method

One hundred twenty interviews were conducted—60 with responders to the "Real cocoa flavor" ad and 60 with responders to the "Take five" ad. Interviewing was conducted among a random sample of respondents to the split-run ads. A three-way chi-square statistic was used to test for differences between the two ads in terms of selected respondent characteristics.

Recommendations and Conclusions

Research advises the use of "Real cocoa flavor"; the latter has respondents who more closely resemble the target market profile. A three-way chi-square shows that respondent profile differences between the ads for sex and (separately) for age are significant.

A higher proportion of respondents to the "Real cocoa flavor" are women (70%) and represent a wider age spectrum.

Respondents to the "Take five" ad are somewhat older. These profile differences are unaffected when age and sex are cross-tabulated; for example, women and men are older for "Take five." See Table 1.

Each ad's respondents do not differ markedly in their experiences with cocoa mixes. A majority of respondents to each ad say that they have never used a cocoa mix product: 60% for the "Real cocoa flavor" ad and 70% of the "Take five" ad. "Real cocoa" draws better from those who are former users of Cocomoco. About 30% of the respondents to the "Real cocoa" ad, compared with 13% from the "Take five" ad, report that they had previously used Cocomoco. See Table 2.

Besides the general reason of just wanting to try the product (about two-fifths of respondents to each ad), "appeal of flavor" (33%) was a frequent mention for "Real cocoa"; no "Take five" respondents mentioned "appeal of flavor." The use of Cocomoco for "cocoa-breaks" was relatively infrequent as a reason for trying Cocomoco ("Take five," 13%; "Real cocoa," 76%). See Table 3.

TABLE 1. Profiles of Respondents to Two "Cocomoco" Ads [a]

Respondents	"Real Cocoa Flavor" (%)	"Take Five" (%)
Profile	$n = 60$	$n = 60$
Females	70	50
Under 50	27	13
50 and over	43	37
Males	30	50
Under 50	20	13
50 and over	10	13

$= 12.95$
$\chi^2 = 1.92; P = $ N.S.
$\chi^2 = 0.86; P = $ N.S.
$\chi^2 = 5.00; P < .05$
$\chi^2 = 5.17; P < .05$

A = sex variable, B = age variable, C = ad variable. N.S. means not significant; $P > .05$.

TABLE 2. Use of Cocoa Mix Brands (before Sending for "Cocomoco" Offer)

Responses	"Real Cocoa Flavor"		"Take Five"	
	Ever Used (%)	Used in the past Six months (%)	Ever Used (%)	Used in the past Six months (%)
Did not use cocoa mix	60	73	70	83
Used cocoa mix	40	27	30	17
Cocomoco	30	13	13	7
Brand A	3	3	7	7
Brand B	3	3	3	—
Brand C	3	3	3	3
Brand D	3	3	—	—
Don't know brand	3	—	3	7
Total	100	100	100	100
Base	(60)	(60)	(60)	(60)

Questions: What brand or brands of cocoa mixes have you ever used before sending for the Cocomoco sample? And in the past six months before you sent for the Cocomoco sample, what brand or brands of cocoa mixes did you use?

TABLE 3. Reasons for Sending for "Cocomoco" Offer

Reasons	"Real Cocoa Flavor" (%)	"Take Five" (%)
Wanted to try it	40	37
Appeal of flavor	33	—
"Cocoa-break"	7	13
To have handy	—	10
Help me relax	17	10
Work or night worker	7	7
Friend recommended	—	7
Dislike other brand	3	3
To give pep	—	3
Saw ad	—	3
Easy to get	—	3
Combat depression	3	—
Don't know	—	3
Total	[a]	100
Base	(60)	(60)

Question: What is your main reason for sending for the Cocomoco offer?

[a] Total exceeds 100% because of multiple mentions.

169

SUMMARY

Advertising quality research determines whether an advertisement attracts consumers to the brand. Research measures consumer recall and perception of an advertisement's messages. It also measures the strength and weakness of alternative advertisements.

Research initially identifies the strongest advertising claim. After this is decided on, research evaluates the effectiveness of different strategies for executing this theme. Knowing the effective way of executing an advertising theme will help insure a strong advertisement.

Once research pinpoints a particular strategy and the execution for the strongest advertising theme, the advertisement is tested in either rough or finished form. The basic criteria for measuring the quality of an ad relate to its ability to generate high recall scores and motivate brand purchase. Campaign advertising tests should be conducted periodically to insure the effectiveness of the advertising over time. The next chapter examines this issue.

It has been learned that advertising quality research serves to guide the development of an advertisement from the initial selection of an advertising theme and execution to the testing of a rough or finished commercial.

It has been learned that advertising quality research serves to guide the development of an advertisement from the initial selection of an advertising theme and execution to the testing of a rough or finished commercial.

TECHNICAL APPENDIX

ALTERNATE DESIGNS FOR ADVERTISING QUALITY RESEARCH

Design Alternatives	Notes
Unit of analysis Category user Category purchaser Company brand user Company brand purchaser	Typically, category purchaser. Company brand purchasers are often a separate unit of analysis when the company brand has a dominant share.
Data collection method Personal Telephone Mail	Personal interview for forced exposure techniques. Telephone for natural exposure techniques and for recall measurement
Stimulus presentation Brand unidentified Brand identified	Invariably brand identified

Design Alternatives	Notes
Consumer criteria Monadic Repeat	Single response, except for prepost advertising response measurement
Evaluation criteria Competitor brands Company brand	Evaluation is certain to use tests of previous advertising for the company brand. Results for competitors also enter into the evaluation of creative products.

ANALYTICAL TECHNIQUES

In this section, we are concerned with chi-square (χ^2) tests of significance. These tests do not assume that the population sampled is normally distributed. Chi-square can be used to test for independence of cross-classifications. The outcome of the test depends on the fit between observed and expected frequencies. All chi-square tests require that (1) observations sum to the total sample and (2) it be completely clear how each observation will be assigned.

Specific techniques treated in this section are two-way ($a \times b$) chi-square, two-way (2×2) chi-square, McNemar's chi-square, and three-way ($2 \times 2 \times 2$) chi-square.

Two-Way ($a \times b$) Chi-Square

The two-way ($a \times b$) chi-square is a between-group technique. Each respondent is classified on a two-way combination of attribute levels. For example, a company may want to test four different kinds of advertising copy for a brand. A design for this test might call for random assignment of each respondent to one of the advertising copy exposure cells. After seeing the assigned copy, a respondent might be asked to select one of three prelisted brands. The result would be a 4×3 matrix. A two-way ($a \times b$), chi-square test would indicate whether there are differences between the four kinds of copy in the ways they relate to brand choice.

This technique may be used as an approximate, quick test of significance when one variable is score. Score data can be converted to class data to meet chi-square test requirements. Chi-square tests are less sensitive for detecting significant differences than are analyses of variance. If the effects are sufficiently strong, use of chi-square is justified when score data are involved.

Analysis 8.1. "Rescue" Shoe Waterproofing Product

In Case 8.1, Rescue, three different advertising claims for this brand were tested. Respondents were blue-collar workers who had worn working shoes in the past month—an important market segment. Each respondent was shown one Rescue claim and one for a leading competitor. Preference between Rescue and the competitor was measured after exposure to the pair of claims. Significance of differences in brand preference was tested by a two-way (3 × 2) chi-square. Differences were found to be significant, and the strongest Rescue claim was recommended.

Two-Way (2 × 2) Chi-Square

The two-way (2 × 2) chi-square is a special case of the two-way ($a \times b$) chi-square. In the former, each respondent is assigned to one of four combined attribute levels. These levels are formed by cross-tabulating two dichotomous nominal variables. An example would be the 2 × 2 matrix formed by (1) assigning individuals to one of two copy approaches and (2) subclassifying these peoples' postexposure selections or nonselections of the brand in the copy. Note that nonselections are recorded systematically, as well as selections.

The two-way (2 × 2) chi-square can use a "correction for continuity." This adjustment reflects that the chi-square distribution is continuous. A fourfold table chi-square is a discrete and crude approximation. The result of the correction is a shrinkage of the original chi-square. In practice, conclusions usually are unaffected by the correction procedure. In addition to the basic test of independence, it is possible to conduct a second chi-square test for the equality of the two proportions.

Analysis 8.2. "Solo" Sugar Substitute

In Case 8.2, Solo, two copy lines for a TV commercial were tested. Respondents were exposed to one of two copy lines and then given the choice of the advertised product or cash. A two-way (2 × 2) chi-square was found to be significant. Inspection of the data showed which copy line was superior.

McNemar's Chi-Square

McNemar's chi-square is a within-group technique. It is appropriate to use McNemar's test for count data that are dichotomous, and the same variable is measured on two correlated samples. This means that a single sample may be measured twice or that matched (or correlated) samples are each measured on the same variable and compared. A company might be interested in stimulating repeat sales of their product from radio advertising. Two radio commercials could be exposed to pairs of respondents matched for brand loyalty, heaviness of product use, and stage of purchase cycle. Which member of each pair receives which treatment would be the result of a random, within-pair selection process.

McNemar's chi-square is used because when samples are correlated the straightforward chi-square is inappropriate; the null hypothesis would be accepted too frequently. Cochran's test is appropriate for count data when there are more than two matched samples.

Analysis 8.3. "Downy-Q" Quilt

In Case 8.3, Downy-Q, respondents were asked twice for their preferences for Downy-Q and another brand: preferences were asked before and after exposure to a test commercial. McNemar's test showed that significant shifts took place, favoring Downy-Q. This provided the necessary assurance to use the tested commercial.

Three-Way (2 × 2 × 2) Chi-Square

The three-way (2 × 2 × 2) chi-square can be used for various design strategies: between, repeat (three measures, one variable), and "mixed" (repeat and between measures). Four null hypotheses are tested with this design: the interaction hypothesis and three hypotheses concerning the two-way associations of variables. An example of a three-way (2 × 2 × 2) chi-square with a mixed design would be a prepost commercial test of buying preference—a two-level nominal variable. The test would be analyzed separately for females and males.

When interaction is present (i.e., three-way, overall chi-square is significant) the interpretation of each additional significant chi-square must be qualified. Data must be studied to understand the meaning and relative importance of each two-way chi-square in these cases.

Analysis 8.4. "Cocomoco" Cocoa Mix

In Case 8.4, Cocomoco, two print ads were tested for differences in sex and age profiles of ad responders who sent for Cocomoco samples. The test design was a three-dimensional (2 × 2 × 2) between layout. A three-way, chi-square analysis was performed on the interrelationships of the three different qualitative variables. No interaction was found in the analysis. This led to the straightforward conclusion of profile differences between ads, based on the significant two-way chi-squares that were found. Thus a reliable decision could be made about which ad to select.

COMPUTER ANALYSIS

A chi-square analysis (2 × 2 case) is presented in this numerical analysis. It is intended to test for association between variables.

Analysis Plan: Chi-Square (2 × 2)

Four classifications are described by the cross-tabulation of two-level variable A with two-level variable B. Twenty respondents have been distributed to these four cells, each respondent to one cell only. Referring to Table 8.1, lines 1–4 give the meanings of the four numerical entries in each cell. "Frequency" indicates the respondent count; "percent," the percentages of the total sample; "row percent" and "column percent," the percentages of the appropriate row and column marginals, respectively. See Table 8.1.

Computer Output

An analysis of the bivariate relationships, using chi-square and several other measures, is found in Table 8.2. The chi-square result and its degrees of freedom and probability level are displayed on the first line. Several other statistics are presented to deepen the interpretation: lines 2, 3, and 4 provide measures of the degree of relationship between the variables. These three

TABLE 8.1.　Chi Square

```
CHI  SQUARE  -  (SAS  BATCH)


                       TABLE  OF  A  BY  B

        A                    B

1       FREQUENCY |
2         PERCENT |
3         ROW PCT |
4         COL PCT | 1          | 2          | TOTAL
        ----------+-----------+-----------+
        1         |         9 |         2 |     11
                  |     45.00 |     10.00 |  55.00
                  |     81.82 |     18.18 |
                  |     81.82 |     22.22 |
        ----------+-----------+-----------+
        2         |         2 |         7 |      9
                  |     10.00 |     35.00 |  45.00
                  |     22.22 |     77.78 |
                  |     18.18 |     77.78 |
        ----------+-----------+-----------+
        TOTAL            11           9         20
                      55.00       45.00     100.00
```

TABLE 8.2.   Chi Square

CHI SQUARE - (SAS BATCH)

STATISTICS FOR 2-WAY TABLES

1	CHI-SQUARE	7.103	DF= 1	PROB=0.0077
2	PHI	0.596		
3	CONTINGENCY COEFFICIENT	0.512		
4	CRAMER'S V	0.596		
5	LIKELIHOOD RATIO CHISQUARE	7.560	DF= 1	PROB=0.0060

measures (phi, contingency coefficient, and Cramer's V) provide a rough indication of the strength of the relationship. Although they are imprecise for interpretation, these measures represent ways of evaluating the extent of the relationship to the degree that each exceeds zero. On line 5, a likelihood ratio chi-square value is shown, together with the degree of freedom on the probability value. Likelihood ratio chi-square is another model that resembles the conventional chi-square. The likelihood ratio computation involves a logarithmic operation. See Table 8.2.

Interpretation

A review of the statistics for two-way tables, in Table 8.2, discloses that a significant association exists between variables A and B. The probabilities for chi-square and likelihood ratio chi-square (0.0077, 0.0060) are highly significant. Three measures of association are given, all of which indicate a moderate interrelationship of variables (phi = 0.596, contingency coefficient = 0.512, Cramer's V = 0.596).

NINE

Marketing Campaigns

The success or failure of marketing campaigns affect product life spans. The research done by you, the researcher, is needed to tell when campaigns have increased the value of a company's product to potential buyers.

In previous chapters, I discussed marketing strategy research, as well as research to improve product decisions and advertising quality. All this is done before commitments are made that can have a telling effect on a brand. This chapter shows how research monitors and evaluates campaigns where they really count—in the marketplace.

"Marketing campaigns" refer to programs for mass selling, sales promotion, or product sampling. The two-month, national airing of a pool of three commercials, based on a common theme, is one example of marketing campaign.

Marketing campaign research tracks consumer behavior that can be traced to mass selling, sales promotion or product sampling. Let's take a look at the research you do that scores marketing compaigns—and how it guides a client or company to take appropriate actions.

Find out how well a campaign worked. The research you do provides information to show how decisively a marketing campaign has affected consumer feelings and actions.

Study results are expected to show if the campaign has led to an improvement in the brand's market acceptance. Has the campaign taken business momentum from competitors? Created brand and category acceptance among noncategory users? Identified the brand with an important benefit?

Criteria of effectiveness vary with the kind of marketing campaign, the measures selected, the timing of measurement, and assumptions about the value of observed changes. In addition, criteria may vary with the stage of a product's life cycle. For instance, criteria, by stages, may shift from informing consumers about the brand to creating brand preferences, to differentiating the brand, and the like.

Before you provide feedback on market response, investigate campaign objectives. Once the objectives are understood, agreement should be reached

176

with management about specific information that indicates whether objectives have been met. You are then in a good position to conduct appropriate research to monitor and evaluate the results.

Inform management about the efficiency of their marketing campaigns. For those campaigns that you recommend, it is desirable that returns be estimated. When this is done, management is in a position to spend in areas of the greatest efficiency—to spend money most profitably for campaigns that pay off. Marketing campaign research leads to better promotional accountability. It improves the advantage to be realized from this part of the marketing mix.

Recommend what to do about test campaigns and existing, large-scale campaigns. In some small-scale tests, several variations of marketing campaigns may be under consideration: different products in a line might be sampled, or two advertising media schedules might be tried out. The task you have is to evaluate study results; you must recommend the one best way of proceeding with a campaign.

Sometimes you are asked to evaluate the results of a single, large scale campaign. With your data, you advise management whether to continue or plan the campaign's termination.

Regardless of the outcome of the evaluation, research is expected to provide feedback. You assist management, through your research, by providing direction for planning future marketing campaigns.

The recommendations you make for test and large-scale campaigns are among the most important you make. The major research problems you face when you evaluate campaign efficiencies appear in Exhibit 9.1.

EXHIBIT 9.1   Examples of Marketing Campaign Problems

Research Problems	Marketing Stimulus— Type of Consumer Purchase
Checking whether an advertising campaign is working	Claims—trial
Testing to see if a sampling program is paying off	Free product—repeat

These examples of marketing campaign problems can be distinguished by whether campaigns (1) use claims to induce trial or (2) distribute free products to stimulate repeat buying. Let's probe further into each of these problems.

CHECKING WHETHER AN ADVERTISING CAMPAIGN IS WORKING

Advertising's effects are subtle. It is not known offhand whether an ad campaign is doing what is expected from it. Therefore, special kinds of research are necessary. To do this research, you, the researcher, measure and then analyze data that help evaluate an advertising campaign.

The research you do analyzes a campaign's performance. Research signals the need for the development of new advertising. It is used to tell management when the time has come to use a back-up ad campaign. When a new campaign seems to be working, you are asked to explain why.

Advertising campaign research isolates the effect of advertising. Sales measures usually are inappropriate for measuring the results of advertising campaigns. Sales reflect the total marketing effort, including product quality and pricing. For this reason, sales can be insensitive to changes in the advertising program. Worse yet, sales trends actually can be misleading when evaluating advertising. For instance, a sales decline because of poor economic trends can take place, despite a very strong advertising campaign.

What measures, then, are best for use in advertising campaign research? Standard measures for this kind of research are total brand awareness (unaided and aided brand awareness combined), brand attitude, brand trial, and brand advertising awareness (claimed and proved). Nonstandard measures can be important, too.

Advertising campaign research measures advertising's performance against specific criteria. These criteria are discussed up-front in advance of the research. Criteria vary by product type. Showroom visits might be used for measuring the performance of an auto manufacturer's advertising, first-time trial for the performance of a paper plate manufacturer's advertising.

The interpretation of results must take into account (1) the spending level of the campaign and (2) the amount of time the advertising has had to create effects. Higher spending for longer time periods generally will lead to stronger, more favorable results.

Results from a brand's advertising campaign are compared to those for other brands in the same product category. For an established product, advertising campaign results are compared to those obtained for previous campaigns. When good results come in, a campaign can be continued or repeated. If the advertising is working, attention may shift to other problems in a brand's marketing.

Case Preview: "Write-On" Felt Markers

The research discussed subsequently in Case 9.1 was implemented to measure the strength of a new advertising campaign for Write-On Felt Markers. Previous research had shown that this brand's image was weak in the marketplace and a new campaign was recommended. The specific objective of the research was to determine if brand image ratings were significantly higher after exposure to the new campaign (over a course of time) and whether brand share increased at all. This study was important on another level. This campaign was recommended by an advertising agency that ran a high risk of losing the account.

The research concluded that brand image ratings significantly improved over the course of the campaign. This campaign was recommended, and the agency retained the account.

Case 9.1   Impact of "Write-On" Felt Marker's Graffiti Campaign

Objectives

The Graffiti campaign for Write-On felt markers was designed to show the extraordinary versatility of this pen. The campaign stressed versatility as a key to the overall quality of the pen. The study aim was to learn if the campaign resulted in an improvement in the brand's quality image.

Method

The Graffiti campaign was run on television for three months in Omaha, Nebraska. Average weekly Gross Rating Points (GRPs) were 150. GRPs are a description of the total impression weight of advertising—without taking audience duplication into account. For TV, GRPs represent gross coverage of TV homes.

Interviewing was conducted by telephone at two time points: (1) the week just before the campaign began and (2) the week right after the campaign ended. Each sample was independent of the other. Both were selected by random digit dialing of Omaha, Nebraska, telephone extensions. Qualified respondents were users of felt markers. The sample size for each phase of interviewing was 500 respondents.

Recommendations and Conclusions

Write-On is the only brand to improve its overall quality image during the Graffiti campaign.

On a seven-point rating scale, Write-On has improved by .25 rating points, over the course of the campaign. A test shows this improvement to be significant. The campaign is found to be highly successful, based on results for the key measure of overall quality. See Table 1.

Pre- and postcampaign respondents to the Graffiti campaign study were given favorable and nonfavorable choices for nine image measurements. They were asked to report the choices most closely associated by them for each of six brands.

Write-On has outperformed all competitors in favorable choices for five of nine categories of felt marker preferences and performance characteristics; this speaks well of Write-On's Graffiti campaign. The categories are "best," "sharp," "proud to own," "modern," and "clean." The results were favorable for all nine categories in which Write-On was measured. See Table 2.

TABLE 1.   Overall Quality Rating of Felt Marker Brands

| Brand | Mean Rating | | t Values |
	Precampaign	Postcampaign	
Write-On	4.05	4.30	4.72 [a]
Brand A	3.90	3.84	1.10
Brand B	3.72	3.68	0.95
Brand C	3.52	3.52	0.50
Brand D	3.42	3.37	0.91
Brand E	2.61	2.53	0.33
Base	(500)	(500)	

[a] $P < .01$.

Write-On's share of felt markers acquired increased over the time the campaign ran. Shares for other brands did not show changes of consequence. Write-On's share increased from 18.0 to 24.6%. Brand preference for Write-On increased over the month-long campaign as well. See Tables 3 and 4.

TESTING TO SEE IF A SAMPLING PROGRAM PAYS OFF

In the measurement of an advertising campaign, you, the researcher, analyze trends as the campaign progresses. With sampling program studies, the sample product, however, is withheld from a random group of eligible consumers. A group receiving the product sample is then compared with the nonsampled (control) group. Fieldwork takes place at a predetermined time after the product samples have been distributed. In other words, in sampling program research, measurement takes place at one time point, and two groups are compared.

Payoff is the criterion for going forward with a sampling program. In sampling programs, the product is the communication. The result is that use of the sample product will lead consumers to make buying decisions fairly promptly. Sampling response is a blunt process, unlike advertising response. Therefore, the study you do centers on differences in brand purchase in sampling program research. You pay less attention to subtle measures, such as brand awareness.

Sampling program research requires that you measure "conversion," meaning the extra percentage of buyers resulting from the distribution of product samples. Payoff calculation uses (1) the conversion measure, together with (2) estimates of the value of a converted customer. The gross value of the sampling program is weighed against program costs. A policy decision is made over the time required to break even or for payback. You recommend sampling programs when an acceptable payoff appears likely.

Information about product use-up and purchase cycles is helpful in measur-

TABLE 2. Imagery of Felt Marker Brands

Image	Write-On		Brand A		Brand B		Brand C		Brand D		Brand E	
	Pre	Post	Pre	Post	Pre	Post	Pre	Post	Pre	Post	Pre	Post
Proud or ashamed to own	5.50	6.64	5.90	5.94	5.79	5.97	5.29	5.41	5.38	5.47	4.23	4.20
Pretty or ugly	5.49	6.59	5.79	5.77	5.71	5.82	4.15	4.27	5.24	5.29	3.92	4.08
Modern or old-fashioned	5.34	6.52	5.61	5.71	5.31	5.56	5.56	5.50	5.21	5.43	4.37	4.39
Best or worst	5.25	6.46	5.59	5.68	5.58	5.64	5.28	5.41	5.09	5.17	3.99	3.93
Smooth or scratchy	6.27	6.31	5.79	5.98	5.50	5.55	5.75	5.86	5.39	5.33	4.84	4.71
Clean or dirty	6.09	6.26	5.56	5.67	5.38	5.48	4.83	5.00	5.19	5.30	4.31	4.52
Keep or lose	6.08	6.25	5.56	5.64	5.57	5.73	4.62	4.78	5.21	5.24	4.13	4.13
Durable or fragile	6.05	6.09	5.45	5.57	5.30	5.35	5.77	5.87	5.11	5.13	4.60	4.66
Sharp or dull	5.81	5.90	5.61	5.56	5.51	5.44	5.13	5.19	5.23	5.31	4.67	4.71
Base	(500)	(500)	(500)	(500)	(500)	(500)	(500)	(500)	(500)	(500)	(500)	(500)

TABLE 3.   Felt Marker Most Recently Acquired

Brand	Precampaign (%)	Postcampaign (%)
Write-On	18.0	24.6
Brand A	8.9	7.9
Brand B	6.9	5.6
Brand C	50.2	51.0
Brand D	2.3	2.3
Brand E	3.3	2.7
Base	(500)	(500)

TABLE 4.   Brand Preference for Felt Markers

Brand	Mean Rank [a]	
	Precampaign	Postcampaign
Write-On	3.32	3.54
Brand A	3.02	3.02
Brand B	2.89	2.86
Brand C	1.95	2.02
Brand D	2.64	2.55
Brand E	1.42	1.40
Base	(500)	(500)

[a]Ranks were inverted so that a brand ranking No.1 received a 6, and so on.

ing conversion caused by product sampling. The timing of the interviews is critical in sampling program evaluations. The validity of the study you do depends on an interviewing schedule that (1) permits sufficient time for use-up of the sampled product and (2) allows time for the respondent to purchase the sampled brand within the typical purchase cycle. Prior information on use-up rates and purchase cycles can be used to plan the timing of interviews. When you do not have this information, you may question random subsamples of respondents about the stage of product use and purchase they have reached. When the time is appropriate, the full-scale study can begin. If care is not taken on interview timing, the study can underestimate or confuse the true conversion rate.

Case Preview: "Just Breathe" Nasal Decongestant

This research (for Case 9.2 that follows) was conducted to measure the success of a sampling program, including the relative effectiveness of "sample only" versus "sample and 25¢ coupon." Previous sampling programs were not successful, based on required payoff level measures. The researcher designed a study to measure the relative success of the two sampling approaches in terms of conversion and payoff levels.

The brand manager had recommended this sampling program after considering several. She was confident that this sampling program would be successful and was disappointed to learn that the test sampling program failed to achieve the required payoff level. The program, nevertheless, was implemented. The brand manager was convinced that the research had understated the sampling program's potential. Unfortunately, the brand's profitability plummeted after a massive investment in the large-scale sampling.

Case 9.2   "Just Breathe" Nasal Decongestant Sampling Program

Objective

Harry Stassal Company mailed 20,000 six-tablet sample packettes of Just Breathe nasal decongestant to three selected markets shortly after Christmas. The receipt of these samples coincided with the peak of the advertising program for January.

The purposes of this research were three:

To measure the effectiveness of the sampling program in terms of the possibility of a payoff and its probable magnitude.

To collect information on brand and advertising awareness and the extent to which sample triers recommended the product to others.

To evaluate the effectiveness of the enclosed 25¢ coupon in stimulating the purchase of Just Breathe Nasal Decongestant.

Method

The sampling program was conducted among two groups: one group was sent a 25¢ coupon with the sample product; the other group was sent the sample product only.

Marketing estimated that such a sampling program on a national basis cost $673,000 and would pay off over a period of two years if more than 7.9% of those sampled would be induced to purchase the product. With a 25¢ coupon, the payoff level reached 9.1% for the two-year period. Past research indicated that purchase among eligible respondents not sampled was 3.8%. Based on this assumption, a Z test of proportions for the payoff hypothesis was planned.

The survey was conducted by telephone among three groups of respondents:

309 who were sent a sample only.

303 who were sent a sample plus a coupon.

189 who were sent neither a sample nor a coupon (the control group).

Recommendations and Conclusions

Purchase of Just Breathe nasal decongestant by sampled respondents reaches 5%. The same 5% purchase rate is found in the sample only and sample, plus coupon groups. Study data confirm an expected 4% purchase level among nonsampled respondents. It is recommended that the Stassal sampling program for Just Breathe be dropped from further consideration. The sampling program fails to achieve the required payoff. A Z test of proportions is presented for sample only and sample, plus coupon alternatives. For both alternatives, the test shows that the results are significantly below required payoff levels. See Table 1.

Although sampling as a method of promoting purchase of Just Breathe falls below the 7.9 and 9.1% payoff levels, sampling does have favorable effects on the brand in terms of (1) increasing brand and advertising awareness and (2) stimulating a word-of-mouth recommendation of the brand to others outside the household.

On an unaided basis, the awareness of Just Breathe nasal decongestant is highest (18%) among respondents receiving the sample, plus coupon, than either among respondents receiving the sample only (10%) or among nonsample respondents (5%).

On the basis of total brand awareness, aided and unaided, sampled respondents report a slightly higher level of brand awareness for Just Breathe nasal decongestant than do the nonsampled respondents (76% for both sample only and sample and coupon versus 68% for the nonsampled group). This level of awareness for Just Breathe nasal decongestant is comparable to that of brand B (78%, 75%, and 77% for each group, respectively) and below that of brand A (98%) in each group.

Similarly, advertising awareness of Just Breathe nasal decongestant is higher than for brand B but well below that of brand A. See Tables 2 and 3.

TABLE 1.   Purchase Interest of "Just Breathe," Brand A, and Brand B

Brand of Nasal Decongestant Purchased	Received Sample Only (%)	Received Sample Plus Coupon (%)	Received Nothing (Control) (%)
Just Breathe	5 [a]	5 [b]	4 [c]
Brand A	28	26	26
Brand B	9	11	11
Base	(309)	(303)	(289)

Question: Have you, or anyone in your household, purchased———?

[a]Significantly below 7.9% payback ($z = 2.07, P < .05$).
[b]Significantly below 9.1% payback ($z = 2.56, P < .01$).
[c]Not significantly different from expectation of 3.8% ($z = 0.17, P = $ n.s.).

TABLE 2. Brand Awareness for Nasal Decongestants

Brand Awareness	Percentage Receiving:		
	Sample Only	Sample Plus Coupon	Neither
"Just Breathe"			
Nasal Decongestant			
Total awareness	76	76	68
Unaided	10	18	5
Aided	66	58	63
Brand A			
Total awareness	98	98	98
Unaided	52	52	38
Aided	46	46	60
Brand B			
Total awareness	78	75	77
Unaided	3	6	5
Aided	75	69	72
Base	(309)	(303)	(289)

Questions: What is the first brand of nasal decongestant that comes to mind?
What is the next brand that comes to mind?
Have you ever heard of the following nasal decongestants?

About 5% of the sampled respondents, both those given coupons and those not given coupons, recommend Just Breathe nasal decongestant to others outside their households. By contrast, none of the nonsampled respondents recommends the products to others outside his household. See Table 4.

SUMMARY

Marketing campaign research tells management when a campaign succeeds or fails. Research monitors campaign performance over time. The results are analyzed for changes in a brand's marketplace performance—changes that relate to mass selling, sales promotion, or product sampling.

Research charts a campaign's success or failure and estimates campaign efficiency and recommends what to do about a campaign. It suggests when campaigns should be expanded, continued, or dropped. The result is improved accountability of a brand's marketing expenditures.

Advertising campaigns and sampling programs are two kinds of marketing campaigns. Advertising and sampling require mass market effort, sustained over time. Advertising's effects, however, are subtle and cumulative. Sampling programs, when the product is the communication, are more likely to show quick and clear indication of buying response.

Advertising campaign research serves to (1) analyze campaign performance,

TABLE 3. Comparisons of Brand and Advertising Awareness

Brand and Advertising Awareness	Sample Only (%)	Sample Plus Coupon (%)	Neither (%)
"Just Breathe" Nasal Decongestant			
Brand awareness (aided and unaided)	76	76	68
Advertising awareness (aided)	56	64	56
Brand A			
Brand awareness (aided and unaided)	98	98	98
Advertising awareness (aided)	80	85	88
Brand B			
Brand awareness (aided and unaided)	78	75	77
Advertising awareness (aided)	46	53	57
Base	(309)	(303)	(289)

Questions: What is the first brand of nasal decongestant that comes to mind?
What is the next brand of nasal decongestant that comes to mind?
Have you ever heard of any of the following nasal decongestants?
Have you seen or heard any advertising for any of the following nasal deconges-tants?

(2) isolate advertising's effect from other variables, and (3) show whether campaign performance meets the criteria.

Sampling promotion studies (1) estimate program payoff (return versus costs) and (2) measure the conversion of customers to the brand.

Decisions about advertising quality affect what creative efforts are used in an advertising campaign. The selection of specific commercials, print ads, and so on, is important for a campaign. But advertising campaign research results reflect, in addition to creative work, media scheduling, advertising weight, and competitive advertising activity.

TABLE 4.   Incidence of Recommendation of "Just Breathe" Nasal Decongestant to Others Outside Household

	Respondents Receiving:		
Responses	Sample Only	Sample Plus Coupon	Neither
Recommended Just Breathe nasal decongestant to others	5	4	—
Did not recommend Just Breathe nasal decongestant	25	32	2
Don't know or no answer or refused	4	2	2
Base	(209)	(203)	(189)

Question: Have you recommended the use of Just Breathe Nasal Decongestant to anyone outside your household?

The success of sampling programs depends on product performance. A sampling program is recommendable to management when the product to be sampled is distinctly superior to its competitors.

TECHNICAL APPENDIX

ALTERNATE DESIGNS FOR MARKETING CAMPAIGN RESEARCH

Design Alternatives	Notes
Unit of analysis Category user Category purchaser Company brand user Company brand purchaser	Typically, category purchase. Company brand purchase is often a separate unit of analysis when the company brand has a dominant share
Data collection method Personal Telephone Mail	Typically, telephone and with independent samples; advertising campaign studies use trend analysis. Product sampling studies usually compare test and control in an "after-only" design

Design Alternatives	Notes
Stimulus presentation Brand unidentified Brand identified	Invariably brand identified
Consumer response Monadic Repeat	Single measures of individuals, although there are usually several criteria
Evaluation criteria Competitor brands Company brand	For advertising campaigns, performance changes in market awareness and receptivity are compared between the company brand and its key competitors. For product sampling, postsampling period purchases are estimated to see if there is a sufficient net increment.

ANALYTICAL TECHNIQUES

This section introduces the simplest tests of hypotheses: (1) two samples, with a score-level-dependent variable, and (2) one sample in which a count is the only variable.

Both of these tests are based on sampling distribution theory. Sampling distributions are the distributions of summarizing measures from equal-sized samples of a universe. Mathematically derived estimates of the variability of the means for such samples are the key to tests of simple hypotheses.

This section covers the *t*-test for independent samples and hypothesis testing for a proportion.

t-Test for Independent Samples

As the name indicates, the *t*-test for independent samples applies to between-group designs. This test is used when respondents are allocated to one of two groups. Each subject is measured once on a score level dependent variable. An example might be a test of the effects of two different advertising campaigns that are run in separate areas. If random samples of target consumers are drawn from each area, a *t*-test for independent samples can be done. This test would lead to the rejection or acceptance of a null hypothesis (i.e., that sample means are from the same universe and do not truly differ). The dependent variable might be scaled ratings of brand leadership.

The previously discussed completely randomized ANOVA (see Chapter 5) is a generalization of the *t*-test for independent samples. In fact, $F = t^2$. It is useful to gain familiarity with both ways of tackling the issue of significance. This facilitates the use of available routines for testing and versatility in ways of expressing results. The t-ratio involves the difference between sample means, divided by a statistic, the "standard error"—the expected variance of the sampling distribution of differences between means.

Analysis 9.1. "Write-On" Felt Markers

In case 9.1, Write-On, an advertising TV campaign was run for the brand. The aim of the campaign was to improve the brand's overall quality image. Two measurements were taken: before- and after-campaign measures of independent samples of respondents. The dependent variable was a seven-point rating scale of overall brand quality. A t-test for independent samples showed a statistically significant improvement in the criterion during the campaign.

Hypothesis Testing for a Proportion

A single sample is obtained for this test. The purpose of the test is to make estimates of the universe proportion. Then the estimates are compared with hypotheses about the universe to see if they are consistent. As an illustration, consider a manufacturer's liability for an offer of free goods, with the submission of proof of purchase. For such programs, it is important to obtain an early estimate of liabilities and stock requirements. Based on small-scale testing, it is possible to estimate whether such a program is affordable—that is, how likely consumer response is to be below a specified cut-off proportion.

The test calls for taking the difference between the observed proportion and that specified in the hypothesis about the universe. The result is divided by the standard deviation of the sampling distribution of a proportion. The ratio is a Z statistic. The table Z values give the probabilities necessary for accepting or rejecting the null hypothesis.

Analysis 9.2. "Just Breathe" Nasal Decongestant

In case 9.2, Just Breathe, consumers were mailed sample packettes of the product. A payoff criterion was worked out for each of two approaches to sampling. Minimum levels of postsampling purchase incidence for the brand were specified. A hypothesis test for proportions was used to gauge the probabilities of payoff. Neither sampling approach appeared likely to achieve payoff.

COMPUTER ANALYSIS

A t-test for independent samples is illustrated in the numerical analysis that follows. The purpose of the test is to challenge a hypothesis that means are equal for two separate groups of data.

Analysis Plan: t-Test for Independent Samples

Scores are listed for each of the two levels of a nominal variable. The scores represent values on a 10-point scale. There are 20 respondents corresponding to each level (group). Each respondent has been assigned one score. In Table 9.1, on line 1, "observation" (Obs) tells the respondent identification. "Group" indicates to which one of the two independent groups the respondent is assigned. "Response" presents each respondent's score on the rating scale.

Computer Output

Table 9.2, t-Test Procedure, shows the basic summarizing statistics for each of the two samples. These include (from line 1) the mean, standard deviation, standard error, and minimum or maximum scores. The *standard deviation* is a measure of the variability of the sample of observations for each group. The *standard error of the mean* is the standard deviation of a sampling distribution of means. The standard error is derived from the standard deviation: standard error $s_m = s/\sqrt{n}$. *The standard errors, for each group, are pooled to compute the standard error of the difference in means,* $s_{m_1} - s_{m_2}$ (not displayed).

Line 2 shows headings for the t-test results—the t-statistic, degrees of freedom, and the probability of a greater absolute value of t. The t-test results are presented twice. They are presented under an assumption of equal variance and under an unequal variance assumption. Line 3 provides an F test of assumptions about equality of variances to aid in the interpretation.

Interpretation

The mean for group 2 is found to be significantly higher than the mean for group 1 ($\bar{X}_2 > \bar{X}_1$, see Table 9.2). The t-test shows that the means of the two samples would be equal only about 5 times in 1000, based on sampling distribution theory. The assumption of equal variance is found to be warranted, as you can see from an F test.

TABLE 9.1. t Test Procedure

STATISTICAL ANALYSIS SYSTEM

T TEST PROCEDURE

1	OBS	GROUP	RESPONSE
	1	1	10
	2	1	10
	3	1	10
	4	1	10
	5	1	8
	6	1	8
	7	1	7
	8	1	7
	9	1	7
	10	1	6
	11	1	6
	12	1	6
	13	1	6
	14	1	6
	15	1	6
	16	1	6
	17	1	5
	18	1	5
	19	1	5
	20	1	5
	21	2	10
	22	2	10
	23	2	10
	24	2	10
	25	2	10
	26	2	10
	27	2	10
	28	2	10
	29	2	9
	30	2	9
	31	2	8
	32	2	8
	33	2	8
	34	2	8
	35	2	8
	36	2	7
	37	2	7
	38	2	6
	39	2	6
	40	2	6

TABLE 9.2. t Test Procedure

T TEST PROCEDURE

VARIABLE: RESPONSE

1	GROUP	N	MEAN	STD DEV	STD ERROR	MINIMUM	MAXIMUM
	1	20	6.95000000	1.79105967	0.40049312	5.00000000	10.00000000
	2	20	8.50000000	1.50437957	0.33638950	6.00000000	10.00000000

2	VARIANCES	T	DF	PROB > /T/
	UNEQUAL	-2.9635	36.9	0.0053
	EQUAL	-2.9635	38.0	0.0052

3 FOR H0: VARIANCES ARE EQUAL, F'= 1.42 WITH 19 AND 19 DF   PROB > F'= 0.4542

192

EPILOGUE

TEN

Consumer Research and the Product Life Cycle

The wealth of consumer research cases available in this book provides information, training, updating, and a review of the field. These cases show how consumer research can be effective in solving marketing problems.

But to use this book to best effect, you, the researcher, must know how these marketing problems enter into the planning of research programs. Research programs are interrelated series of research projects for individual brands.

Researchers and managers must work together on these programs. They must budget and plan for projects that solve the most important problems facing the brand they are concerned with. How can researchers and managers know which problems, when solved, will have the greatest payoff? The answer, in large measure, depends on where the brand is in its product life cycle.

Needs for marketing information change with the product life cycle—from new product development and introduction through growth, maturity, and even decline. A brand's stage in the product life cycle indicates how consumer research fits into the marketing plan. There are many opportunities to use consumer research to make management decisions in each of the four generally accepted stages of the life cycle of a product.

Regardless of where a product is in its life cycle, it is essential to have answers to these basic questions:

Who are the prospects for this product?
What kind of brand impressions does the product project?
Is the product meeting consumer needs?
Is the product keeping its customers?

In addition, special marketing challenges may arise at any time in a product's life cycle. These challenges often require specific answers through consumer research before decisive action can be taken.

For example, a periodic check is necessary to see whether a brand's advertising is working. When a fresh advertising campaign is needed, advertising pretest research can be extremely valuable.

Here are some research opportunities for a new product launch. A new product often begins as a concept. Consumer research can help to do the following:

Find concepts for new products.
Name brands.
Have new products deliver what their concepts promise.

With the best research design, consumer research sounds out the potential market to reduce risk in the introduction of a new product. Based on research data, go/no-go decisions are reached in the early stages of a product's development. If the decision is "go," consumer research can be used to do the following:

Guide new product formulation.
Make new product quality competitive.
Find packages for new products.
Evaluate advertising claims.
Choose ways to present advertising.
Select the appropriate advertising weight.

Here is the research strategy as a product grows in the marketplace. As market share increases, consumer research can improve profitability. Research in the growth phase can do the following:

Reexamine the target market.
Improve brand loyalty.
Select line extension concepts.

Consumer research can help to monitor and further sharpen the marketing program when a product is in its mature phase. When market share has stabilized, interest centers on promotional strategies to maintain market share. Consumer research is called into play to for these reasons:

To select on-pack offers.
To test the payoff of a sampling program.
To check whether the advertising campaign is working.

Eventually, a product begins to decline in market share. A "harvest" strategy is employed in which resources allocated to the product are minimized, and returns from the product's sales are invested elsewhere.

An effort is made to "revitalize" the product by modernizing it. At this stage, the research you do will help in these areas:

Replace product concepts.

Improve or replace packages.

Decide to change products.

The pages of this book provide the tools necessary to define marketing problems and tell how to solve the problems with consumer research. That is only part of your responsibilities as a researcher. Equally important, you must know not only how to solve problems but also which problems to solve for the products in question.

APPENDIX A

Index to Selected
Analytical Techniques

Technical Appendix of Chapter:	Technique
3	AID
	Discriminant analysis
4	Factor analysis
	Conjoint analysis
5	Completely randomized design ANOVA
	Randomized blocks: repeat measure ANOVA
	Split-plot, between-within ANOVA
	Kruskal-Wallis test
6	Completely randomized factorial two-and-three-way ANOVA
	Completely randomized factorial three-way ANOVA
	Split-plot, between-between-within ANOVA
	Friedman test
7	Randomized block factorial $a \times b \times s$
	Randomized block factorial $a \times b \times c \times s$
	Split-plot, between-within-within ANOVA
	Completely randomized design ANOVA
8	Two-way $(a \times b)$ chi-square
	Two-way (2×2) chi-square
	McNemar's chi-square
	Three-way chi-square $(2 \times 2 \times 2)$
9	t-Test for independent samples
	Hypothesis testing for a proportion

Technical Sources Correlated to Chapters in this Book

| | | Chapter | | | | | |
Source [a]	3 and 4	5	6	7	8	9
Blalock (1972)	—	317–360	—	—	275–316	219–242
Kirk (1968)	— —	99–150 245–282	171–244 283–318	319–422	—	—
O'Muircheartaigh and Payne (1977)	Vol. 1 89–124 221–238	—	—	—	—	Vol. 3 1–34
Sheth (1977)	23–30 51–82 135–162 257–286	—	—	—	—	—
Siegel (1956)	—	184–193	166–172	—	104–111 175–179	—

[a] Page numbers are those of cited sources.

APPENDIX B Refs.

Blalock, Hubert M. *Social Statistics.* New York: McGraw-Hill, 1972.
Kirk, Roger E. *Experimental Design: Procedures for the Behavioral Sciences.* Belmont, Calif.: Wadsworth, 1968
O'Muircheartaigh, C. A., and Payne, C. *The Analysis of Survey Data* (2 vols.). New York: John Wiley & Sons, 1977.
Sheth, Jagdish N. *Multivariate Methods for Market And Survey Research.* Chicago: American Marketing Association, 1977.
Siegel, Sidney. *Nonparametric Statistics for the Behavioral Sciences.* New York: McGraw-Hill, 1956.

APPENDIX C

An Aid to Determine Sample Size

Expected Accuracy of Percentages Observed from an Individual Sample (95% Level of Confidence) [a]

Size of Sample	Expected or Observed Percentage				
	10 90	20 80	30 70	40 60	50 50
100	6.00	8.00	9.16	9.80	10.00
200	4.24	5.66	6.48	6.92	7.08
300	3.46	4.62	5.30	5.66	5.78
400	3.00	4.00	4.58	4.90	5.00
500	2.68	3.58	4.10	4.38	4.48
750	2.20	2.92	3.34	3.58	3.66
1000	1.90	2.52	2.90	3.10	3.16
1500	1.54	2.06	2.36	2.52	2.58
2000	1.34	1.78	2.04	2.20	2.24
2500	1.20	1.60	1.84	1.96	2.00

[a] This table shows sampling errors in data for selected sample sizes and observed percentages. Sampling errors are the same at 90% or 10%, and so forth.

Supplementary Readings

Aaker, D. A., and Day, G. S. (1980), *Marketing Research*, New York: John Wiley & Sons.

Adler, Eric (1978), "The Neglect of Promotions Research During Economic Recession and Expansion or Not Another Coupon Redemption Scheme, Surely?," *Market Research Society Conference*, **4**, 213–220.

Anderson, Rolph E. (1973), "Consumer Satisfaction: The Effect of Disconfirmed Expectancy on Perceived Product Performance," *Journal of Marketing Research*, **10**, 38–44.

Anderson, W. Thomas, Jr. (1971), "Identifying the Convenience-Oriented Consumer," *Journal of Marketing Research*, **8**, 179–183.

Anderson, W. Thomas, Jr., Cox, Eli P., III, and Fulcher, David G. (1976), "Bank Selection Decisions and Market Segmentation," *Journal of Marketing*, **40**, 40–45.

Andreason, Alan R. (1966), "Geographic Mobility and Market Segmentation," *Journal of Marketing*, **3**, 341–348.

Andreason, Alan R., and Belk, Russell, W. (1978), *Consumer Response to Arts Offerings: A Study of Theater and Symphony in Four Southern Cities*, Washington, D.C.: National Endowment for the Arts, RWO-22-6N.

Andrews, I., and Valenci, E. (1970), "The Relationship between Price and Blind-Rated Quality for Margarines and Butters," *Journal of Marketing Research*, **7**, 393–395.

Arnt, Johan (1977), "Laboratory Studies and the Laboratory Paradigm of Man: Confessions of an Uneasy Consumer Researcher, *Journal of Consumer Policy*, **1**, 32–44.

Bagozzi, R. P. (1980), *Causal Models in Marketing*, New York: John Wiley & Sons.

Baker, M. J., and Churchill, G. A. (1977), "The Impact of Physically Attractive Models on Advertising Evaluations," *Journal of Marketing Research*, **14**, 538–555.

Baritelle, J. L., and Folwell, R. J. (1975), "Researching the Wine Buyer," *Wines and Vines*, **56**, 26–27.

Barnes, J. G. (1974), "Factors Influencing Consumer Reaction to Retail Newspaper Sale Advertising," in R. Curhan (ed.), *Proceedings of the American Marketing Association*, Chicago: American Marketing Association.

Bearden, William O., and Woodside, Arch G. (1976), "Interactions of Consumption Situations and Brand Attitudes," *Journal of Applied Psychology*, **51**, 764–769.

Belch, G. E., and Landon, E. L., Jr. (1977), "Discriminant Validity of a Product-Anchored Self-Concept Measure," *Journal of Marketing Research*, **14**, 252–256.

Bettinger, C., Dawson, L., and Wales, H. (1979), "The Impact of Free-Sampling Advertising," *Journal of Advertising Research*, **3** (6), 35–39.

Birdwell, A. E. (1968), "A Study of the Influence of Image Congruence on Consumer Choice," *Journal of Business*, **41**, 76–88.

Blattberg, R., Buesing, T., Peacock, P., and Sen, S. (1978), "Identifying the Deal Prone Segment," *Journal of Marketing Research*, **15**, 369–377.

Brown, F. E. (1980), *Marketing Research: A Structure for Decision Making*. Reading, Mass.: Addison-Wesley.

Brown, F. E., and Granbois, D. (1977), "Factors Moderating the Resolution of Reference Conflict in Family Automobile Purchasing," *Journal of Marketing Research*, **14** (2), 77–86.

Buzzell, R. D., and Wiersemd, F. D. (1981), "Successful Share-Building Strategies," *Harvard Business Review*, **59** (1), 91–102.

Campbell, B. M. (1969), "The Existence of Evoked Set and Determinants of Its Magnitude in Brand Choice," Ph.D. Dissertation, New York: Columbia University.

Cay, R. E., and Bodur, M. (1978), "Consumer Response to Dissatisfaction with Services and Intangibles," in H. K. Hunt (ed.), *Advances in Consumer Research*, **5**, 263–272.

Churchill, G. A. (1979), *Marketing Research: Methodological Foundations*, Hinsdale, Ill.: Dryden Press.

Cotton, B. D., and Baab, E. M. (1978), "Consumer Response to Promotional Deals," *Journal of Marketing*, **42**, 109–113.

Craig, Samuel, C., and McCann, J. M. (1978), "Assessing Communications Effects on Energy Conservation," *Journal of Consumer Research*, **5** (3), 82–88.

Crossley, David J. (1979), "The Role of Popularization Campaigns in Energy Conservation," *Energy Policy*, **7** (1), 57–68.

Czepiel, J. A., and Rosenberg, L. M. (1977), "The Study of Consumer Satisfaction: Addressing the 'So What' Question," in H. Keith Hunt (ed.), *Conceptualization and Measurement of Consumer Satisfaction and Dissatisfaction*, Cambridge, Mass.: Marketing Science Institute.

Davis, K. R. (1981), *Marketing Management* (4th ed.), New York: John Wiley & Sons.

Day, Ralph L. (1977), "Extending the Concept of Consumer Satisfaction," in William D. Perrault (ed.), *Advances in Consumer Research*, **4**, 149–154.

de Burzer, F., and Stapel, J. (1978), "Quality Perceptions (A and B) and Brand Pricing," *European Research*, **6** (2), 57–61.

Dodson, J. A., Tybout, A. M., and Sternthan, B. (1978), "Impact of Deals and Deal Retraction on Brand Switching," *Journal of Marketing Research*, **15**, 72–81.

Dolich, Ira J. (1969), "Congruence Relationships between Self-Images and Product Brands," *Journal of Marketing Research*, **6**, 80–84.

Dommermuth, W. P., and Millard, W. J. (1967), "Consumption Coincidence in Product Evaluation," *Journal of Marketing Research*, **4**, 388–390.

Dornoff, R. J., and Tatham, R. L. (1972), "Congruence between Personal Image and Store Image," *Journal of the Market Research Society*, **7**, 45–52.

Engel, J. F., Blackwell, R. D., and Kollat, D. T. (1978), *Consumer Behavior* (3rd ed.), Hinsdale, Ill.: Dryden Press.

Faison, Edmund W. J. (1977), "The Neglected Variety Drive: A Useful Concept for Consumer Behavior," *Journal of Consumer Research*, **4**, 172–175.

Farley, J. U., and Ring, L. W. (1974), "A Simultaneous Equation-Regression Test of the Howard-Sheth Model," in John U. Farley, John A. Howard, and L. Winston Ring (eds.), *Consumer Behavior: Theory and Application*, Boston: Allyn & Bacon, 205–226.

Festinger, L. (1957), *Theory of Cognitive Dissonance*, California: Stanford University Press.

Fishbein, M., and Ajzen, I. (1975), *Belief, Attitude, Intention, and Behavior: An Introduction to Theory and Research*. New York: Addison-Wesley.

French, N. D., Williams, J. J., and Chance, W. A., "A Shopping Experiment on Price-Quality Relationships," *Journal of Retailing*, **48** (3), 3–16.

Fry, Joseph N. (1971), "Personality Variables and Cigarette Brand Choice," *Journal of Marketing Research*, **8**, 298–304.

Gabor, A., and Granger, C. (1970), "The Attitude of the Consumer to Prices," in B. Taylor and G. Wills (eds.), *Pricing Strategy*. Princeton, N.J.: Brandon/Systems Press.

Gentry, J., and Doering, M. (1977), "Masculinity-Femininity Related to Consumer Choice," *Proceedings of the American Marketing Association*, Educator's Conference, 423—427.

Gintner, J. L. et al. (1981), "The Design of Advertising Experiments Using Statistical Decision Theory: An Extension," *Journal of Marketing Research*, 18 (1), 120—123.

Golden, L. (1977), "Attribution Theory Implications for Advertisement Claim Credibility," *Journal of Marketing Research*, 14, 115—118.

Gronhaug, K. (1973), "Some Factors Influencing the Size of the Buyers' Evoked Set," *European Journal of Marketing*, 7, 232—241.

Gronhaug, K. (1974), "Education and Buying Behavior," *Acta Sociologica*, 17, 179—189.

Grubb, E., and Hupp, G. (1968), "Perception of Self, Generalized Stereotypes, and Brand Selection," *Journal of Marketing Research*, 5, 58—63.

Grubb, E. L., and Grathwohl, Harrison L. (1967), "Consumer Self-Concept, Symbolism and Market Behavior: A Theoretical Approach," *Journal of Marketing*, 31, 22—27.

Hall, M., and Littler, B. (1979), "Brand Image Research to Aid Advertising Planning—A Corny Tale," *Market Research Society Conference*, 3, 99—109.

Hamm, B., and Cundiff, E. W. (1969), "Self-Actualization and Product Perception," *Journal of Marketing Research*, 6, 470—472.

Handy, Charles R. (1977), "Monitoring Consumer Satisfaction with Food Products," in H. Keith Hunt (ed.), *The Conceptualization of Consumer Satisfaction and Dissatisfaction*, Cambridge, Mass.: Marketing Science Institute.

Hansen, F. (1972), *A Cognitive Theory of Consumer Choice Behavior*, New York: Free Press.

Hansen, F. (1976), "Psychological Theories of Consumer Choice," *Journal of Consumer Research*, 3, 117—42.

Holbrook, M. B. (1974), "A Synthesis of the Empirical Studies," in John U. Farley, John A. Howard, and L. Winston Ring (eds.), *Consumer Behavior: Theory and Application*, Boston: Allyn & Bacon, 229—252.

Hooley, G. J. (1979), "Perceptual Mapping for Product Positioning: A Comparison of Two Approaches," *European Research*, 7 (1), 17—23.

Howard, J., and Sheth, J. (1969), *The Theory of Buyer Behavior*, New York: John Wiley & Sons.

Howard, J. A. (1977), *Consumer Behavior: Application of Theory*, New York: McGraw-Hill.

Hull, P. B., and Seydel (1979), "The Role of Market Research in Developing New Products—(Re)searching for Gold," *Market Research Society*, 47—60.

Jacoby, J. (1978), "Consumer Research: A State of the Art Review," *Journal of Marketing*, 42, 87—96.

Jacoby, J., Chestnut, R., and Fisher, W. (1978), "A Behavioral Process Approach to Information Acquisition in Nondurable Purchasing," *Journal of Marketing Research*, 15 (November), 532—544.

Jacoby, J., Olson, J., and Haddock, R. (1971), "Price, Brand Name, and Product Composition as Determinants of Perceived Quality," *Journal of Applied Psychology*, 55, 570—579.

Jeuland, Abel P. (1978), "Brand Preferences over Time," in S. C. Jain (ed.), *Research Frontiers in Marketing*, 43, 33—37.

Johnson, R. M. (1971), "Market Segmentation: A Strategic Tool," *Journal of Marketing Research*, 8 (2), 13—18.

Kamen, J. M., and Toman, R. J. (1970), "Psychophysics of Prices," *Journal of Marketing Research*, 2, 27—35.

Kassarjian, H. H. (1971), "Personality and Consumer Behavior: A Review," *Journal of Marketing Research*, 8, 39—43.

Katona, George (1974), "Psychology and Consumer Economics," *Journal of Consumer Research*, 1, (1), 1–8.

Kerby, J. K. (1975), *Consumer Behavior: Conceptual Foundations*. New York: Dun-Donnelley.

Kinnear, T. C., and Taylor, J. R. (1976), "Psychographics: Some Additional Findings," *Journal of Marketing Research*, 13, 422–425.

Kogan, N., and Wallach, M. A. (1972), "Risk Taking," in J. Cohen (ed.), *Behavioral Science Foundations of Consumer Behavior*, New York: Free Press.

Krugman, Herbert (1965), "The Impact of Television Advertising: Learning without Involvement," *Public Opinion Quarterly*, 29, 349–356.

Landon, E. Laird, Jr. (1974), "Self-Concept, Ideal Self-Concept, and Consumer Purchase Intentions," *Journal of Consumer Research*, 1, 44–51.

Lane, P. F., and Hannah, I. W. (1979), "The Utilization of Research in a Product Advertising Campaign—The Case of Smirnoff," *Market Research Society Conference*, 3, 69–82.

Lavidge, Robert J., and Steiner, G. (1961), "A Model for Predictive Measurements of Advertising Effectiveness," *Journal of Marketing*, 25, 59–62.

Lehman, D. R. (1979), *Marketing Research and Analysis*, Homeward, Ill.: Richard D. Irwin.

Lundstrom, W., and Lamont, L. (1976), "The Development of a Scale to Measure Consumer Discontent," *Journal of Marketing Research*, 13,2 373–381.

Lunn, Tony (1972), "Segmenting and Constructing Markets," in R. M. Worcester (ed.), *Consumer Market Research Handbook*, Maidenhead, Berkshire: McGraw-Hill.

Lussier, D. A., and Olshavsky, R. W. (1974), "An Information Processing Approach to Individual Brand Choice Behavior." Paper presented at the Operations Research Society of America/The Institute of Management Sciences Joint National Meeting, San Juan, Puerto Rico.

McConnell, J. Douglas (1969), "The Price-Quality Relationships in an Experimental Setting," *Journal of Marketing Research*, 5, 300–304.

McGuire, William J. (1977), "Psychological Factors Influencing Consumer Choice," in Robert Ferber (ed.), *Selected Aspects of Consumer Behavior*, Washington, D.C.: U.S. Government Printing Office (NSF/RANN Program).

Maddox, R. N., Gronhaug, K., Homans, R. E., and May, F. E. (1978), "Correlates of Information Gathering and Evoked Set Size for New Automobile Purchasers in Norway and the U.S.," in H. Keith Hunt (ed.), *Advances in Consumer Research*, vol. 5, Ann Arbor, Mich.: Association for Consumer Research, 167–170.

Mason, J. B., and Mayer, M. L. (1970), "The Problems of Self-Concept in Store Image Studies," *Journal of Marketing*, 34, 67–69.

Mauser, G. A. (1980), "Positioning Political Candidates: An Application of Concept Evaluation Techniques," *Journal of the Market Research Society*, 22, (3), 181–191.

Maynes, E. Scott (1976), *Decision-Making for Consumers*, New York: Macmillan.

Mehrotra, S., and Wells, W. D. (1977), "Psychographics and Buyer Behavior: Theory and Recent Findings," in A. G. Woodside, J. N. Sheth, and P. D. Bennett (eds.), *Consumer and Industrial Buying Behavior*, New York: Elsevier North-Holland, 49–65.

Michael, R. T. (1972), *The Effect of Education on Efficiency in Consumption*, New York, Columbia University Press.

Miller, John (1977), "Data Reduction Techniques and the Exploration of Satisfaction Segments," in R. L. Day (ed.), *Consumer Satisfaction, Dissatisfaction, and Complaining Behavior*, Bloomington: Indiana University Press, 102–114.

Miller, S. J., Mazis, M. B., and Wright, P. L. (1971), "The Influence of Brand Ambiguity on Brand Attitude Development," *Journal of Marketing Research*, 8, 445–449.

Mitchell, A. A. (1980), "Cognitive Processes Initiated by Exposure to Advertising," in R. Harris (ed.), *Information Processing Research in Advertising*, Hillsdale, N.J.: Lawrence Erlbaum Associates.

Monroe, Kent B. (1971), "Measuring Price Thresholds by Psychophysics and Latitudes of Acceptance," *Journal of Marketing Research*, **8**, 460–464.

Monroe, Kent B. (1973), "Buyers' Subjective Perceptions of Price," *Journal of Marketing Research*, **10**, 70–80.

Montgomery, David B. (1971), "Consumer Characteristics Associated with Dealing: An Empirical Example," *Journal of Marketing Research*, **8**, 118–120.

Morris, G., and Cudiff, E. (1971), "Acceptance by Males of a Feminine Product," *Journal of Marketing Research*, **7**, 372–374.

Morrison, B. J., and Dainoff, M. J. (1972), "Advertisement Complexity and Looking Time," *Journal of Marketing Research*, **9**, 396–N400.

Munsinger, G. M., Weber, J. E., and Hansen, R. (1975), "Joint Home Purchasing Decisions by Husbands and Wives," *Journal of Consumer Research*, **1**, 60–66.

Narayan, C. L., and Markin, R. J. (1975), "Consumer Behavior and Product Performance: An Alternative Conceptualization," *Journal of Marketing*, **39**, 1–6.

Nelson, James E. (1978), "Children as Information Sources in the Family Decision to Eat Out," *Advances in Consumer Research*, **6**, 419–423.

Nicosia, Francesco M. (1966), *Consumer Decision Processes: Marketing and Advertising Implications*, Englewood Cliffs, N.J.: Prentice-Hall.

Olander, F. (1970), "The Influence of Price on the Consumer's Evaluation of Products and Purchases," in B. Taylor and G. Wills (eds.), *Pricing Strategy*, Princeton, N.J.: Brandon/Systems Press.

Olander, Folke (1977), "Consumer Satisfaction—A Skeptic's View," in H. Keith Hunt (ed.), *Conceptualization and Measurement of Consumer Satisfaction and Dissatisfaction*, Cambridge, Mass.: Marketing Science Institute, 409–452.

Oliver, Richard L. (1979), "Product Satisfaction as a Function of Prior Expectations and Subsequent Disconfirmation: New Evidence," in H. K Hunt and R. L. Day (eds.), *New Dimensions of Consumer Satisfaction and Complaining Behavior*. Bloomington: Indiana University Press.

Olshavsky, R. W., and Grandbois, D. H. (1979), "Consumer Decision Making—Fact or Fiction?" *Journal of Consumer Research*, **6**, 93–100.

Olshavsky, R., and Miller, J. (1972), "Consumer Expectations, Product Performance, and Perceived Product Quality," *Journal of Marketing Research*, **9**, 19–26.

Olson, J. C., and Dover, P. (1979), "Disconfirmation of Consumer Expectations through Product Trial," *Journal of Applied Psychology*, **64**, 179–189.

Olson, Jerry (1977), "Price as an Information Cue: Effects on Product Evaluations," in Arch Woodside, Jagdish Sheth, and Peter Bennett (eds.), *Consumer and Industrial Buying Behavior*, New York: Elsevier North-Holland.

Ostlund, L. Y. (1973), "Evoked Set Size: Some Empirical Results," in T. V. Greer (ed.), *Combined Proceedings, Fall Conference*, vol. 35, American Marketing Association, 759–760.

Parsons, T., and Smelser, N. (1956), *Economy and Society: A Study in the Integration of Economic and Social Theory*, London: Routledge & Kegan Paul.

Pessemier, E. A., Burger, P. C., Teach, R. D., and Tigert, D. J. (1971), "Using Laboratory Brand Preference Scales to Predict Consumer Brand Purchases," *Management Science*, **6**, 371–385.

Peterson, R. A., and Kerin, R. A. (1977), "The Female Role in Advertisements: Some Experimental Evidence," *Journal of Marketing*, **41**, 59–63.

Plummer, J. T. (1971), "Life Style Patterns and Commercial Bank Credit Card Usage," *Journal of Marketing*, **35**, 35–41.

Plummer, J. T. (1974), "Applications of Life Style Research to the Creation of Advertising Campaigns," in W. D. Wells (ed.), *Life Style and Psychographics*, Chicago: American Marketing Association, 167–180.

Pomerance, Eugene (1977), "Generalizations from Accumulating Copy Test Results," *ESOMAR Congress* Oslo, 199–215.

Punj, G., and Staelin, R. (1978), "The Choice Process for Graduate Business Schools," *Journal of Marketing,* **15,** 588–598.

Raju, P. S. (1977), "Product Familiarity, Brand Name and Price Influences on Product Evaluation," *Proceedings, Association for Consumer Research,* Seventh Annual Conference, 64–71.

Raju, P. S., and Hastak, M. (1980), "Consumer Response to Deals: A Discussion of Theoretical Perspectives," in Jerry C. Olson, (ed.), *Advances in Consumer Research,* vol. 7, Chicago: Association for Consumer Research.

Rao, V. R. (1972), "Marginal Salience of Price in Brand Evaluations," in M. Venkatesan (ed.), *Proceedings of the Association for Consumer Research,* Chicago: Association for Consumer Research.

Ray, M. L., Sawyer, A. G., Rothschild, M. L., Heeler, R. M., Strong, E. C., and Reed, J. B. (1973), "Marketing Communications and the Hierarchy of Effects," in P. Clarke (ed.), *New Models for Mass Communications Research, Vol. II, Sage Annual Reviews of Communication Research,* Beverly Hills, Calif.: Sage.

Robertson, Thomas S. (1976), *Consumer Behavior,* Glenview, Ill.: Scott-Foresman.

Robertson, Thomas S. (1976), "Low Commitment Consumer Behavior," *Journal of Advertising Research,* **16,** 1976, 19–24.

Robinson, P. J. (1968), *Advertising Measurement and Decision Making,* Boston: Allyn & Bacon.

Sands, Sal (1979), "Techniques for Creating New Product Ideas," *Management Decision,* **17,** (2), 202–213.

Schlinger, M. J. (1979), "A Profile of Responses to Commercials," *Journal of Advertising Research,* **19,** (2), 37–46.

Schneider, Kenneth (1977), "Prevention of Accidental Poisoning through Package and Label Design," *Journal of Consumer Research,* **4,** 67–74.

Semenik, R. J., and Young, C. E. (1979), "Market Segmentation in Arts Organizations," in Neil Beckwith et al. (eds.), *1979 Educators' Conference Proceedings,* Chicago: American Marketing Association, 474–478.

Sharir (Sraier), Shmuel (1974), " 'Brand Loyalty' and the Household's Cost of Time," *Journal of Business,* **47,** (1), 53–55.

Shoemaker, R. W., and Shoaf, F. R. (1977), "Repeat Rates of Deal Purchase," *Journal of Advertising Research,* **14,** 47–53.

Silk, A. J., and Urban, G. L. (1978), "Pre-Test-Market Evaluation of New Packaged Goods," *Journal of Marketing Research,* **15,** 171–91.

Simon, Marjii F. (1970), "Influence of Brand Names on Attitudes," *Journal of Advertising Research,* **10,** 28–30.

Sproles, George (1977), "New Evidence on Price and Product Quality," *Journal of Consumer Affairs,* **11,** 63–77.

Srivastava, R. K., Shocker, A. D., and Day, G. S. (1978), "An Exploratory Study of Situational Effects on Product Market Definition," in H. Keith Hunt (ed.), *Advances in Consumer Research,* Ann Arbor, Mich.: Association for Consumer Research, 32–28.

Steiner, G. A. (1980), *Strategic Planning: What Every Manager Must Know,* New York: Free Press.

Stewart, D. W. (1981), "The Application and Misapplication of Factor Analysis in Marketing Research," *Journal of Marketing Research,* **18,** (1), 51–62.

Swan, J., and Comb, L., "Product Performance and Consumer Satisfaction: A New Concept," *Journal of Marketing,* **40,** (2), 25–33.

Szybillo, George (1975), "A Situational Influence on the Relationship of a Consumer Attribute to New-Product Attractiveness," *Journal of Applied Psychology,* **60,** 652–655.

Szybillo, G. J., and Jacoby, J. (1972), "The Relative Effects of Price, Store, Image and Intrinsic Product Differences on Product Quality Evaluation," in M. Venkatesan (ed.), *Proceedings of the Association for Consumer Research,* Chicago: Association for Consumer Research.

Triandis, H. (1981), "Attitudes and Interpersonal Behavior," in D. Levine (ed.), *Nebraska Symposium on Motivation,* Lincoln: University of Nebraska Press.

Troutman, C. M., and Shanteau, J. (1976), "Do Consumers Evaluate Products by Adding or Averaging Attribute Information?," *Journal of Consumer Research,* **3,** 101–106.

Tull, D., Boring, R., and Gonsier, M. (1964), "A Note on the Relationship of Price and Imputed Quality," *Journal of Business,* **37,** 186–191.

Tybout, A. M., Calder, B. J., and Sternthal, B. (1981), "Using Information Processing Theory to Design Marketing Strategies," *Journal of Marketing Research,* **18,** (1), 73–79.

Vitz, P. C., and Johnson, D. (1965), "Masculinity of Smokers and the Masculinity of Cigarette Images," *Journal of Applied Psychology,* **49,** 155–159.

Webb, P. H. (1979), "Perceptual Discrepancies in the Time Duration and Number of Television Commercials," in W. Wilkie (ed.), *Advances in Consumer Research,* vol. 6, Ann Arbor, Mich.: Association for Consumer Research.

Webster, Frederick E., Jr. (1965), "The 'Deal Prone' Consumer," *Journal of Marketing Research,* **2,** 186–189.

Wells, W. D. (1975), "Psychographics: A Critical Review," *Journal of Marketing Research,* **12,** 196–213.

Wells, W. D., and Tigert, D. J. (1976), "Activities, Interests, and Opinions," *Journal of Advertising Research,* **11,** 27–35.

Wells, W. D., Andriuli, F. J., Goi, F. J., and Seader, S. (1957), "an Adjective Checklist for the Study of 'Product Personality,'" *Journal of Applied Psychology,* **41,** 317–319.

Westbrook, Robert A. (1977), "Correlates of Post-Purchase Satisfaction with Major Household Appliances," in R. L. Day (ed.), *Consumer Satisfaction, Dissatisfaction, and Complaining Behavior,* Bloomington: Indiana University Press, 85–90.

Wilke, W. L., and Pessemier, E. A. (1973), "Issues in Marketing's Use of Multi-Attribute Attitude Models," *Journal of Marketing Research,* **10,** 428–441.

Wind, Yoram (1973), "A New Procedure for Concept Evaluation," *Journal of Marketing,* **37,** (4), 2–11.

Wind, Y., and Green, P. E. (1971), "Some Conceptual, Measurement, and Analytical Problems in Life Style Research," in W. D. Wells (ed.), *Life Style and Psychographics,* Chicago: American Marketing Association, 97–126.

Winer, R. S. (1980), "Analysis of Advertising Experiments," *Journal of Advertising Research,* **20,** (3), 25–31.

Winter, F. W. (1975), "Laboratory Measurement of Response to Consumer Information," *Journal of Marketing Research,* **12,** 390–401.

Wittink, D. R., and Cattin, P. (1981), "Alternative Estimation Methods for Conjoint Analysis: A Monte Carlo Study," *Journal of Marketing Research,* **18,** (1), 101–106.

Wolgast, E. (1968), "Do Husbands or Wives Make the Purchasing Decisions," *Journal of Marketing,* **23,** 151–158.

Zajonc, R. B. (1968), "Attitudinal Effects of Mere Exposure," *Journal of Personality and Social Psychology,* Monograph Supplement, **9,** 1–27.

Zand, D. (1981), *Management in a Knowledge Society,* New York: McGraw-Hill.

Index